Collection:

MY PRACTICES NOTEBOOK

Teje-Má

Book 1

THE MASTER PLAN

Susi Calvo

THE MASTER PLAN

My practices notebook - 1

Susi Calvo

Translated from the Spanish by Norma Torres and José María Lozano, in Queretaro, Mexico.

Library of Congress Control Number: 2012919371
ISBN: Softcover   978-1-4633-2568-8
                         Ebook   978-1-4633-2569-5

This book was printed in Spain.

English translation by Mª Asunción Jovani

To order additional copies of this book, contact:
Palibrio
1663 Liberty Drive
Suite 200
Bloomington, IN 47403
Toll Free from Spain 900.866.949
Toll Free from the U.S.A 877.407.5847
Toll Free from Mexico 01.800.288.2243
From other International locations +1.812.671.9757
Fax: +1.812.355.1576
orders@palibrio.com
427482

CONTENTS

THIRD PART
"CURRENT TIME"

DEDICATION

This book is dedicated to the Creator of this universe, thanks to him we can make our practices here.

It is dedicated to all the elohims, to all the creators beings that people this planet. I hope you enjoy my occurrences and wake up your remembrances to take them with you as we leave this wonderful universe. And, above all, that they will help us make our own universe, one day.

It is dedicated to the ascending humans… for the purpose of using these teachings in the "Ascension". Here we have come with a lot of entities to help them in this transit, who should not hesitate in grabbing our offered hand.

It is dedicated to Trixi and Taaron… My two most proximate elohimic colleagues. Well… I mean, to the wonderful: Rafa and Fabri.

To Rafa's woman and kids: Ananda, Cristian, Sofia, Nauk.

Also to the human family that I still have… The Javi, the Pepi, the Albert, the Montse, my aunts, uncles and cousins, also the Silvia, the Maribel, the Dóniga.

To Rafa, Samuel, Aníbal, and Aura, and all the De Horna plus all their children.

To all the gang who is around me all this time…

Wonderful and genial colleagues, from which I quite learn: Mireia, María, Josep, Titania, Varen, Reyes, Javi, Lore, M. Antonia, Antea, Chema, Pingo, Niam, La Mari, Emilia, Alba, Chon, Jaime Seg., Pablo, Isabel, Pascual, Fernando Parr., Clara Yaneth, Aralanda, Roberto S., Marìa José, Miyo, Sarabjit, Claudia R., Kartar, M.Carmen G. Erbandé, Conxi Vila., Goran, La Mercé, Silvina, Silvia M., Alana, Ana Blesa, Danijela, Eli Alfaro, Maribel Parrilla, Karim y many more…

And to all their little children:. Judit, Axail.la, Raquel, Yava, Amara, Diego, Daniel, Andrés, Ulises, Ákkara, Valeria, Constanza, Ana, Isabel, Alejandro, …

And more and more kids than I have been finding…

To Titania,.. who is doing a big job with my "base body", mating with it in its journeys.

I also dedicate to all who read it… hahahahaha…

And I hope you enjoy it very very much… hahahahaha…

What I mean is…

I dedicate it to you… with all my love…

Enjoy it !!!!!

Teje-Ma. Ávila January-20, 2012

ACKNOWLEDGEMENTS

To whom I have to acknowledge the most is to Sarabjit.

She has been the impulse of this piece. If she had not proposed me this edition, I would have not finished it and it would have been in a drawer for a year.

I also acknowledge to all who have read it and told me how they liked it... That's good!!!... This has really motivated me to continue writing this collection...

Susi

FOREWORD

Susi takes us to a walk around the galaxy through an enthusiastic and innocent just graduated Elohim's view.

The journey begins without a break and with a smile in the lips. A magnificent stellar excursion through the space beyond limits. A rapid pilgrimage that comprehends from the most elevated Elohim's conscience to the hard landing of our ass hitting the Earth.

The main character, Teje Maneje, light and full of humor as his author, makes himself lovable while trespassing borders from different worlds, while living a series of covers progressively denser. The story is centered in the different stages and dimensions that he has to descend, like it would be a ladder to go down all the depth of the well in the Matrix we live. And then on, he continues without rest until that conscience gets to control a human body, like yours or mine, and gets it with master.

The book is about genetic memory. You have to recall that your way through the multiuniverse and stop believing that you are sand trying to elevate from mud.

We come from the heart of the Great Spirit and have descended to matter-life. This is a novelistic history that each of us lives (descending beings in the most part), as we arrive the first time to this planet. The internal path that forced us to increase the density of our vehicles (going through an airplane, fast boat, car, bike, to this tricycle which image we contemplate at the other side of the mirror), and all this to conquer the right to step consciously the green robe of the goddess.

Many stories, varied potentials, different gifts...

The Elohims make their way from Orvonton to Nebadon, passing by very variable jobs and learning to manage their external senses and to interrelate with the four elements. Galaxies, stars, planets...They start to manage the DNA and continue with their contacts in more elevated dimensions, up to the moment in which the planet is set in quarantine caused by Lucifer's rebellion. Now our Elohim (up to the moment living in a subtle fourth dimension body) is forced to incarnate through a human belly, and to continue doing it until he achieves to exit the Samsara (Matrix) illusion.

TejeMa gets together with his divine spark Taaron and both travel the incarnation wheel, and evolving with games of feeling and willing as well as loving female and the power of male. Finally, at this time, Susi incarnates in her own body, and writes the story that we have in our hands. There are no available powers any more, all the subtle fails, and it is necessary to strive a lot to help others to advance in their inner path.

Little by little the quarantine softens, specially in this last quarter of century (1987-2012) that beings from high dimensions incarnate to help with individual and planetary ascension. And it makes possible to reincarnate in ourselves, make descend the divine Being that we are to this body, until the Spirit illuminates each cell, until "the Sun that lives in shadows", from the ancient Vedic rishis, illuminates and this body be able to be the perfect vehicle for the Elohim that I Am. For this, we need a resistant body, conscious, without hiding shadows, with an ego in service of the Being and a Sun shinning in our heart.

And it is in this final stage, that it tells Susi's personal story, after her first awakening in 87, and in 90 when I met her. In 92, I think, while I was celebrating the "Heart awakening of Hispania", with thousands of persons in Santiago de Compostela's Cathedral. After a long pilgrimage with eldery mexicas, she participated in the Visions Counsel of Segovia in 93 (the last public act of the "Nanita" in Spain, since she flew to wind freedom in March 94). And since then, with Arael, we established a brotherhood that has not been broken.

It is for me a great honor to present this book collection (it is quite clear that this doesn't end here) and I am sure that they would make you reconsider about the long descending way that we travelled to get to live in this Goddess' body. The different stages that we have been creating, all the kingdoms of the mother Tonantzin, before trying the genetic changes with the arbor-monkey that was neardhental, guardian in its blood of a genetic library of many light galactic races.

THE 2012 will be history soon, but it will leave a footprint in our opened hearts, of lighted children that will incarnate, of the genetic and brain changes through solar electromagnetic storms, and the multidimensional consciousness which will allow us remember this kind of stories as the one that I introduce you.

Bon voyage to each of you!

Miyo

Miyo and Susi
(Alcover, Tarragona- SPAIN – June, 2012)

PRESENTATION

"FROM THE SPHERES"

Hi, my name is Tejemaneje, but you can call me Teje-Ma.

I am an elohim, which means... a Creator Being, dedicated to creating things... giving them life.
We are also called "cosmic engineers".

I live in a sphere of the **"Internal Circle"**.

I am a Being made of Light and a thin layer similar to the skin, (so as to have a shape).

You cannot see me because your eyes do not perceive my Vibratory Frequency.

My mates and me, can enter one inside each other, go through each other and play in that way.
Our world is different from yours, but I will use our similarities for your understanding.
I am here with my mates, practicing. I am creating a planet with rings around it, can you see it?
Yes, I am the one in the middle.

Very soon, we will go to worlds inhabited by creations and we will become part of them, in order to live the experience of being the creation of an Elohim.

Our professors say that in order to learn how to create "in perfection" it is necessary to be and to live like they do, many, many lives.

Experience everything that we can and become conscious of it, registering everything in our memory.

That's why I will tell you my story,,, as if I were writing a practicejournal,,, hahahahaha.

Come with me to other worlds... come... join me in this trip...

I will show you how things are seen from my eyes, the eyes of an elohim.

FIRST PART
"IN THE UNIVERSE"

In this section, I am going to tell you what has happened to me since I left home, until I arrived to your planet and started interacting with humans

CHAPTER 1

"THE DESCENT"

<u>HAVONA. Central Universe</u>
(For further explanation of these concepts refer to: "The Urantia Book", in the section about the universes and similar topics).

I am very excited, because we have just finished the theoretical classes, and today we will be assigned the place where we will do practices...
Here at my side, I have Taaron, my soul mate. He's younger than me, but he is learning very fast.
The teacher is coming... let's see what he tells us..

> I will write the teacher's sentences in *italics* with a point and dash before. I'll write point and dash before the phrases that we say, but in regular font so that you can distinguish these from my own reflections which will not have any notation before, is that clear? Hahahahahaha. Well... here it goes...

.- Today is your last day of classes.

My classmates twitch in their seats, they are nervous, they are anxious to end the theoretical classes.

The teacher is also very happy that finally he has finished his task with us.

.- Tomorrow, you will be assigned the universe where you will practice the lessons learned here. You will find your kindred souls, and all of you will descend to places with a greater energetic density than here. You will need other bodies, other vehicles, which will be more adequate to each dimension. Have you understood?

.- Yes, yes, yessss…

We are so excited with this field trip, that we don't pay any attention to the teacher.

Making a comparison with your planet, it would be the same as, after having attended classes for nine months, we were now to leave for summer camps, to practice everything we have learned here, but in a "survival" mode. I guess you like summer camps? Of course!!

.- Teje Ma!!!…Teje Ma!!!

.- What do you want Taaron?

.- To which universe do you think they're going to take us?

.- I don't know, but for sure we'll have a good time.

.- I'm eager to leave!

The next morning:

*.- My dear little elohims, - says the Dean of this study center–
are you prepared to begin this trip?*

We are jumping and jumping, impatiently.

*.- We will first divide you in
groups, because there are
quite a lot of you. We are
going to form "Practices
Teams". All the members
in each group will go
together to the same place,
there you will be separated
to practice individually.*

*That will happen in
different places of the
same universe. When you have accomplished the practice
tasks, the team will meet for prepare its return. Do you
understand?*

Here I am showing you my "Practice Team" mates …
Do you know which one is me?..hahahahaha

Don't we look a little bit alike?

The teacher continues:

*.- You will be supported and guided by specialists at all time.
Sometimes you may see them and talk to these guides, at
other times, they will be invisible, so that you feel free to act
your way.*

The Dean introduces the guides who will take us to our respective universes and they each summon their groups.

We are very attentive to meet our guide. When we already know who he is, we walk up to him and we group with all the sparks that will travel with us, "the team" assigned to number 51.

We hug, and enter each other, we traverse each other... We feel the emotion!

Descent to the Superuniverse.

In Team 51 we begin to receive the instructions to descend to the next level.

Another guide comes, -there is one for each step we take-. Every time we change frequencies we change guides.
They take us from one place to the other. They are the ones who have permission and the frequency to enter those places. We can't go alone. On one hand, because we would not know where to go; and on the other, because we may lose or go into places where we are not supposed to go.

*.- Hi, I am your guide, my mission is to take you to **UVERSA**, capital of the 7th Superuniverse named **Orvonton**.*

.- Every time you descend to a lower level than the precedent one, you will have to create a cover, an adequate body for that level. The body that you will be using in that place to relate with other beings belonging to that level. Is that clear?

.- Yes, yes, yesss.

.- Because your elohimic shape is so subtle, so transparent, that if you show yourselves with it in another place, nobody could see you; therefore, you couldn't relate, nor exchange expressions or ideas. Do you understand?

How annoying,,, he's repeating the same thing over and over, as if we didn't know how things work. Look, what he is teaching us now, … I will compare it to something you know in your planet, so that you may understand.

Do you remember those dolls that open up and a smaller one appears inside? I think you call them "matriuskas". They have different shapes. Some have a woman outside and a man inside for example. I will give you some images…

One suit goes inside another one. I will be the smallest, the one who is contained by all the other ones. But I will also be the most "powerful". Hahahahaha… who leads them all from the inside.

Well, let's see what else this guide tells us.

.- Well, now your practices start. I invite you to prepare the suit for entering the Superuniverse. Go ahead! Let's see what you have learned.

He shows us some body models for this place. I invoke the subtle energy, I grasp it with my little hands and compress it making it denser and connecting it with the dimension frequency of the place we are descending to. In this way, little by little, with the power of my thoughts, and with my hands I build a vehicle, a body, a cover, a suit (or however you want to call it) similar to the sample.

It is like when divers put on their black suits to go deep into the ocean. They move very well inside their suits. Even though it's a little bit suffocating... isn't it? And it doesn't work when they are outside the water.

We have two possibilities when making our suit, one is to make it outside and then try it on, and the other is to make it on top of ours, like a sticker... hahahaha.

Taaron looks at me and copies my actions.

.- Do you have your vehicles?

.- Yes, yes, yesss

.- Well, put them on, we are leaving.

We get inside our little suits and follow our guide.

*.- Now you will join 144,000 others and you will be part of one entity, which we call **a monade**. In this way it will be much easier to travel through the ethers.*

We do as he says and we don't seem to be so many.
For your understanding, it is like a group of cells joining to build an arm of a body. We are many cells, but we build only one arm. For sure you understand.
And when the arm moves, we all move... Hahahaha... it's very funny! Like in a roller coaster!... Hahahaha... Like we are doing the wave!

The trip is short. We have the sensation of climbing on a cloud and feel the wind on our faces while we descend to another energetic level...

.- We are arriving to the Superuniverse. Prepared to enter its capital?

We stop at the entrance gates.

.- Well, now you have to behave very good, be silent and be good, because we will introduce ourselves to the "practices chiefs", but we have to ask for permission to get in first.

The guide steps away from the group for a moment and goes towards a group of beings who control the entrance and exit of entities from the Superuniverse.
It's like **customs**.
Here they check who enters or leaves and where she/he goes. They have everything very much under control.
It is always necessary to ask for permission when you arrive to a new place.

Once the entrance permit is granted, the guide returns to the team accompanied by a guiding-entity who will take us before the corresponding Hierarchy.

The guiding-entity introduces himself, as we walk with him he comments:

.- You know that any place you go to, your energy will have an influence, you will not be able to go unseen because you come from higher levels of consciousness and therefore, you have greater power, wisdom, love and other energetic qualities than any being that inhabits the place that you

will be assigned to practice. So you have to be cautious and humble. Try to learn rather than show off your skills.

Finally we reached the entity that represents the practices Hierarchy.

.-Welcome, my mission is to assign you to a practice place that will be interesting for you. We have looked for an area that will bring forth situations in which you may practice what you have learned in the Spheres of the Central Universe, where you inhabit. You will be directed to the star of Sirius, which belongs to the Nebadon Universe. In that place you will be given adequate instructions and the situation will be explained.

.- But now we'll take you for a tour of this place so that you can learn some things.

.- Hey… Teje-Ma

.- Tell me Taaron.

.- What do you know of the Nebadon Universe?

.- Well, let's see… let me remember… I know it's a new universe. Its creator is called Mikael from Nebadon.

.- Hey… Teje-Ma… and … When we get to that universe and we assume the bodies from that place will our **"consciousness be clouded"**?

.- Well it depends on where we are and what our tasks are. But remember that it is in our own benefit. In this way we won't be thinking of anything else except learning or simply … in … SURVIVING! … which is enough!! Hahahaha…

.- And how will we meet? Will we recognize each other somehow?

.- Relax, relax,... One thing that we will feel is a sensation of being before someone we somehow already know, and it is due to the profound energy that we send out, noticeable in the fire in our gaze. When we see each other we'll say:... "you look familiar... but I don't know where from"... Hahahaha.

.- But... we'll be close by... Won't we?

.- Yes, of course! Remember what we have been told before: those who are part of the same monad always are together. So, you and me will not be separated. We will be very close.

The guide addresses the group ...

.- *How was the visit?...Have you learned a lot? Someone wants to tell me about Sirius?*

.- Yes, me, Trixi
Well... Sirius is one of the spiritual centers of one area of the Nebadon Universe. It oversees 28 Great Systems, from a managing point of view. I imagine we will go there because it is a great study center. It is a base, an enormous university, where high level beings join to teach us and also to mentor us while we go to the Systems to practice.

.- Since very wise beings live there, it is also a place where beings from elsewhere come for advice.

.- *Very well, we know a little bit more of the place we are going to, don't we?*

.- Yes, yes, yessss …

.- *Well, assume denser matter than the current one, provide it with Sirius's frequency and build your vehicles. Are you ready?*

So we get concentrate on making up our Sirius suits.

.- Hey Taaron, I will name my Sirian vehicle.

.- Really? How are you going to call it?

.- Danae… what about you… How are you going to call yours?

.- Well.. yes… let me see… I will name it Vondeas.

On the side the voices of other elohims are heard…

.- Well I will name it… Deamska…

.- And I…Ainde…

.- Well me, Varen.

.- Well I like the name… Dekan-Seina,.. said by a lovely voice.

All of us laugh at our occurrences… a few others baptize their vehicles.

CHAPTER 2

"ADAMS AND EVES"

<u>In one planet of this galaxy:</u>

.- Taaron come one moment.

.- What's up Teje Ma?

.- Look, I am pregnant again.

.- Uuups…We are in trouble! We have been warned too many times!!!

.- That happens to us because we love each other and we like to make love, we enjoy it a lot. It is something very special because it links us to our divine side.

<u>For you, who are reading this:</u>

I think you are not getting anything, are you?

I will update you.

When we were taken to Sirius, we were assigned tasks.

For Taaron and me, the task we were given was what you would call "Adam and Eve". The objective is to go to a planet inhabited by souls in primitive forms, animal shaped, wear a cover with their shapes and have children.

Those born from us, mix with the indigenous inhabitants and conform a more intelligent generation, with a different way of thinking, with new ideas and emotions.

In this way, we help them climb a step in their evolution process.

It means that they take an evolutionary leap thanks to us.

But, here where we are we adopt two shapes. One is that of the indigenous and a different shape in private. (Two different "covers").

We have a place for us, a closed precinct, private, where we use bodies that are more comfortable and luminous, in order to rest, feel freer and regenerate a little.

In these other bodies we are not allowed to have relations which result in pregnancies, as it would destabilize the planet, (if these children came into contact with them). But well… you see… I'm pregnant again!

Now, I don't know what is going to happen because we already have several children in this private place.

And I can see they want to go out of the precinct. Just what we need!!!

Visit from Practice Chiefs:

A little bit serious.

.- *We specifically asked you not to have relations when not in the indigenous form. And you have not complied. We have to take away the creatures that don't belong to this planet. And we will see what the consequences are, the karma. Please be more careful!...*

.- And what are you going to do with them?

.- *We'll take them to the ships and educate them as pilots. Is that OK?*

.- Yes, yes. Perfect!

They left, taking the little ones with them.

Buff... At least they were not that harsh!! We'll see what karma will be like!...

.- Look Taaron, we have to try not to be so loving, otherwise we'll have a bigger problem each time, hahahaha...

.- But, we have been in other planets playing Adam and Eve and haven't had a problem!

.- Because we didn't have two possible pregnancies. We only had the primitive shape of the planet. Now that we have more possibilities and comfort, we are failing... I am sure we need to learn some kind of lesson.

The one of following the rules, for sure!

We are being little rebels. Hahahahaha

.- Anyway, I think we have enough children in many planets, maybe it's time to be apart… Don't you think?…

.- Yes, let's request that we change practices, just when we are done here. Let's see which kind of task we are given…

.- Mmmmmm… I don't like much the idea Teje-Ma… You know that we're better when we are closer… eh???… Hahahahaha…Should we go inside?…

.- You never stop Taaron… Hahahahaha… Come on, come on…!!! Hahahaha.

CHAPTER 3

"DANAE"

In my Sirian ship:

Well... here I am, alone, practicing.

In my current form, named Danae.
I will tell you what it is like, according to your parameters.
You would see: A male shape: tall, muscled, elegant, very good looking, serious, in a ship commander suit.
Blond hair, "prince" hair style.
Very luminous, slanted eyes,
Approximately 25-30 years.

I am in the 12th dimension.
The issue of dimensions is also difficult to understand...
You have already gone over the lesson that "nothing is still, everything vibrates",... well everything can vibrate or move, faster or slower. The faster it moves, the harder it is for the human eye to see the object.

Like the propellers of a plane. When they move very fast, you know they are there, because you saw them when they were at a stand still, but when they move quickly, you can't see them any more.

That's how my cells move, very very quickly, at high speed,,, therefore, you would not be able to see me.

The speed of movement has to do with the spiritual elevation, the more spiritual an entity is, the higher his vibration is.

That also has to do with the worlds you inhabit... There are worlds that require bodies with a higher vibration and others with a slower vibration, which will be denser. Slower or denser are related with being "more primitive".

I am currently planning to create a planet.

I will put in it all kinds of animals, plants, people and other things.

I create the design, and then I look for an expert team who turn it into reality. They materialize it. They will build the elements according to the design I am planning.

I have asked Mika, this universe's creator, to be my mentor on this creation. I am waiting for his answer, it would be a great honor for me.

A few beings of a small height, blue skin, very similar to elohims but from the Sirian dimension enter the room. They are my assistants.

.- ¡Danae!!…. ¡Danae!!…

.- ¿What's up?

.- The Creator is calling for you. He asks you to go to the "communication room".

I arrive to the indicated place and I enter very respectfully.

.- Beloved Creator.

.- *Dear Danae.*
I received your request to be mentored by Myself.
I appreciate your deference.
And… let's begin.

.- *In the first place, you will address the Sirian Eldery*
Counsel, where you will be assigned a new task.
I want you to practice in various places what we call the
"Evacuation Plan", in other words, when an inhabited
planet has some kind of trouble, the population needs to be
rescued, a group of entities takes care of this, I want you to be
a part of these teams. I am sure you will learn a lot.

.- Thank you so much. Beloved Creator.

I took my leave with great respect and a joyful sensation, and at the same time I think of the responsibility of this task.

I feel tickles in my belly (if I had a belly, of course).

CHAPTER 4

"EVACUATION PLANS"

I am still in Danae's body, but am now in the "Star" ship, which belongs to the **"Intergalactic Confederation"**, formed by a group of leaders from 33 worlds that have common objectives.

It is a **mothership**.

It is very big, like a small planet.
Many beings of different shapes, sizes and dimensions live here.

We are in charge of security for these 33 worlds.
We protect them from disasters, enemy attacks, and other things.
We also collaborate with the Hierarchies in their petitions, and if in our hands, about the planets' evolution.

In the topic of evacuation plans, we work in teams. My task here is **rescue**. When a disaster happens and we realize that humanity in a planet won't survive in its totality, we pick them up and make them safe.

At least in enough numbers for repopulation.

There are some groups that take the form of a places' bodies and are in charge of warning the people to be prepared. My team is only responsible of planning. But, at some point, I would like to take part of those who assume a body there. It is much riskier and problematic. But... for sure it is very interesting.

If this is the case, you have to inhabit the planet from the beginning of its creation in order to leave footprints in the places where it is safe, if there are any. Mark them in some way.

In the next occasion, I would like to live this adventure. It has to be very exciting...!

Today, I am happy because I have been very well received in Sirius, as we have successfully finished the Fourth Evacuation Plan.

I have gone through 4 planets and we have achieved to save many people.

In the first planet, a **meteorite rain** was fulminating everything.

As we can see what is going to happen, we planned a new place for the inhabitants and before the meteorite rain came, they were already in that other planet that we had prepared in advance.
We began transferring them little by little, with time.
They helped a lot, even though it was hard for them to believe what was going to happen.

In the second planet, it was **water** which caused the disaster. Everything was flooded, the inhabitants were left without homes, crops, and the place became inhospitable.
What we did here was to take the people to our ships and held them there for some time until the water descended and the planet was habitable again.
These people were more suspicious and not until they had water to their necks, did they believe.
It is more difficult to rescue them when this happens.

The third one was a planet with very primitive inhabitants. The land was formed by islands.
The volcanoes erupted.
We had to put the indigenous to sleep, by means of wave emissions, from our ships and then take them to another planet.
The islands sank and there was no food for them. They would have died burnt by the acid rain and then, had any be left, they would have starved.
Luckily enough there were just a few and things were not that hard.
They are happy now and glad in a new place, full of food that they can enjoy.
And they are not completely aware of what happened.

For the fourth world we had to enable caves and other intraterrestrial spaces because **the air became unbreathable** in the surface, creating illnesses and mutations. It took us a while to enable everything, but we were successful in saving a lot of people. They have stayed in these caves because they are very comfortable there, they have everything they need and it will be a long time before the air in the surface becomes breathable again.

Well… I am ready for the next one.

I rub my hands while thinking that I am doing things correctly and that my practice chief is happy with me.

This makes me happy... who wouldn't be?

SECOND PART

"MY CONNECTION WITH PLANET EARTH"

I have already been called for the **fifth evacuation plan**. It is going to be in your planet.

This time I am going to assume the shape of a human body…

Maybe I will end up rescuing you!…

Uyuyuyuy…. So exciting!

Before telling you my adventure in The Earth, I tell you what happened previously, so that you'll be able better understand what comes next.

CHAPTER 5

"The Neighboring Planets"

The Earth, your planet, at the beginning was a mass that slowly took its current shape, with mountains, valleys, water, vegetation, ...etc...
But I guess that was already clear for you... hahahaha...

The neighboring planets were inhabited. Venus as well as Maldek.
The latter, which you also call Malona was destroyed and became an asteroid belt which lays between Mars and Jupiter.

In Maldek, people were very much alike to people currently living on the Earth.
The evolutionary characteristics are very similar.
In that planet I lived several lives. I learned quite a lot.
Ambition and lust for power resulted in advanced technology weapons being used without limits, and the planet was destroyed.

The inhabitants who could be rescued, passed on to Venus.

I have several memories from Maldek, but the one that I recall the most is about the life I shared with Taaron. Who I have been running into.

He was in the military and had secret plans.

I was a spy for the opposing side and… his lover!

I had to steal the plans from him. I put my hand inside the safe box where he kept them but he had set a trap.
A guillotine fell over my wrist and cut off my hand.
Fortunately medical technology was very advanced and it could be replaced!
But I never forgot the shock.
I still glance ever so often towards my left hand to check if it's still there… hahahahaha…
The truth is that it is a super nasty and shocking sensation. Can you imagine?

In Venus we were able to evolve a lot.
It is the planet of love, as you very well say.
And we learned about it quite well: Love in all of its extension.

I will share another memory from Venus, of a life with Taaron.

My body for that place was a tall, blond, beautiful and sporty girl. I remember very well having my long hair up in a pony tail, which moved rhythmically while I was exercising.

I had just entered the Air Force Academy, where I would be prepared to fly combat ships. Technology was very advanced. We had ships to go to space, although they couldn't go very far yet.

I met Taaron's body when I was running through a training camp. He had made himself a very nice body too.

He had enrolled the Academy, just like me. But we hadn't met each other.

While I was running, I noticed a group of young men and his smile made him outshine everyone else. From my point of view, of course!

At the Academy, I felt like he was looking for me, he sat by me any chance he had, but he would not talk to me.

At a party, as I was tired of his shyness, I asked him to dance. As soon as we embraced, we realized there was something going on.
Of course, our consciousness was clouded and we didn´t know what was happening, but… the attraction energy made us not want to let go of each other throughout that whole life.

After a while, a team of young people was formed with the mission to explore The Earth.
We presented ourselves as volunteers and we came to do the research of the place. We flew small ships. And we accompanied expert biologists and other scientists. We were like a small army that chauffeured and protected the scientists.

At first, only we, the explorers, went in couples to explore various areas of the planet, taking back a lot of data for the experts who saw the possibility of travelling themselves and bringing life here.

A great experimental lab was organized in the area that is today called Jericó. In the current land of Israel.
We began to bring animals to experiment how they would adapt to the place.

The majority of this group of Venusians were my mates from "Practice Team 51".
One of the anecdotes is that Dekan-Seina was assigned to quite gently bring eggs of different species.

And I laugh, because I remember she mixed up eggs of the different species in the same nest, as some of them were predators, at birth, they ate the others. She had to start all over again… but she learned a fun lesson. Even though some of the scientists were not very happy and she put on some karma on her back… hahahahaha… And everything because she did what she thought was best, without following scientists' directions,… hahahahaha…
Another little rebel!!!!

The DNA codes of a monkey species were transformed and they evolved very quickly.
Immediately, the difference among these and the non transformed was very noticeable. They became "humanoids".

I stayed on these labs for a while and learned to handle DNA.
Of course,,, because under the pilot cover, I was wearing the "cosmic engineer" one…
And the energy inclines you towards your origins.
I felt like fish in water!!!

After some time, after returning from the Earth exploration, Taaron, in his Venus body, and myself in mine, had three children.

I was very much marked by watching his death. A devise that exploded, destroyed him. My children and me saw this sequence closely. I was in shock for a long time. When events are so traumatic you remember then life after life after life. So it is better to have our consciousness clouded. Otherwise.......there are so many traumas from so many lives,,, that no one would want to be reborn again, don't you think?

I'll continue telling you about Venus:

As a planet, it evolved too, and went from one dimension to the next.
We were living in the fourth dimension, for you, it would be a very subtle world. Transparent.
More or less like ghosts live... hahahaha...
Trespassing walls and people... hahahaha...

But Venus has already passed to the fifth dimension, a mental world, of fire.

Not all of its inhabitants were able to pass because they hadn't evolved enough.
So, lower level beings descended to the Earth, to become a part of it, in its third dimension.
Those who passed to the fifth dimension went to higher worlds.

It is like moving through school grades. As the school with your grade -fourth dimension-, no longer exists in Venus... hahahaha... you have to attend another school, Planet Earth, you are sent to a lower grade and you have to climb from a lower level. It is necessary to make a bigger effort.

But, for sure you know a bit more than those that are currently in such level. You could even help them and everything!

Venus, is left to rest, for now. You know that everything is relative, and time even more.

There were also elevated beings that voluntarily came to the Earth, to help souls that undergoing this process.

Normally, when a planet increases its vibratory frequency, the entities that inhabit it also have to change their frequency; otherwise, it is impossible for them to stay there. The energy itself expels them.

The Earth is going through the same process.

The planet in itself, as an entity, also evolves and passes to another dimension.
The beings that are living in it, either pass with it, or have to leave to other places where they are comfortable.

CHAPTER 6

"THE BEGINNING OF THE END"

Even though these things have happened a long time ago, I will talk to you **in the present tense,** as it is easier for me to remember them like that.
In this way, you will feel as if you were present when they happened.

Currently I am in a body called **Ebanne**, it is female.
Taaron, is in a male body called **Van**. We are a couple.
We are in the Earth, your planet.
We have been for quite a while here.

When we ended our lives in Venus, we went to our practice chiefs and they sent us to other planets to continue evolving.
Some of us were in planets belonging to the Pleiades.
Mainly in the "blue world" and the "green world", which are very similar to the Earth.
I have a memory that I will tell you about. Hahahaha…

Taaron was a prince in one of his lives in the "blue world", they lived like you did here in the medieval age.

I was female, and was in a different and highly evolved planet, I drove a small spaceship and did tourism, visiting several planets, curious as always.

Traveling, traveling,… I ended up in the world where Taaron was… hahaha… and we always end up meeting each other… don't we?… That's how things are!…

He was galloping a spirited blue horse (in a blue world… that's the color of some horses)… and I thought that was very funny. I followed him with my spaceship.
Discretely at first, more openly later. He had not seen inhabitants from other worlds nor seen any spaceships.
I placed my spaceship in front of him and he was surprised. The horse became very nervous, it threw him to the ground and kept running.
I descended from my spaceship and went to help him.

We were together for a good amount of time.
First, it was strange,… surprising,… but little by little we got used to each other and recognized each other.
Additionally, we didn´t speak the same language and that was a little bit annoying, as well as the differences in our bodies and our level of evolution.
For some time, we had clandestine dates, until he asked to come with me for a ride.
And… he didn´t come back to his planet. All that was left was a legend of "the prince that was taken from the skies", told by the elderly to the children of the place… hahahaha…

Currently, a numerous entity group, has been sent here to the Earth to collaborate with the inhabitants' evolution.
We have come in couples.

Our bodies have a very similar structure to human bodies, so that they are not scared of us, yet we are handling ourselves in the third and fourth dimensions.

When we are with the inhabitants we become denser and stay in the third dimension. When we interact amongst us, we do so in the fourth dimension, subtler and easier for us.

The majority of us are a part of Team 51.

I'll tell you how things are around here: There is a large number of inhabitants in the Earth.

We are like technicians: we give advice, support, ideas.

Each couple has formed a group, some teach agriculture, some to hunt, also to make some devises, to heal wounds with herbs and things like that.

Van and I teach how Justice works.

He is very passionate and holds a lot of interest in complying with the guidelines we've set forth.

We teach how to live with respect and harmony.

Some stand out for their qualities and we are preparing them to be group leaders. The idea is not for us to do everything, on the contrary, it is to prepare them to be independent and free.

I focus more on women and Van in men.

We like to promote equality and equilibrium among them.

We gather them and talk about their problems. Sometimes, men and women on their own and some others all together.

Human settlements have been formed in different places of the planet. We travel with our transportation from one place to another.

Our group has a leader who is the "Planetary Prince". He is very active, passionate and feels like a free being.
"Planetary Prince" is a position. It can be held by whom is prepared for it. Like a career. It is not necessary to be from Royalty.

I will assign the Planetary Prince an invented name, because I don't have his permission to use his true name here.
I will call him… let me see… Ahmmm… CAL-GIS.

Well CAL-GIS met some days ago a leader that commands several Systems, whom I'm going to call LUMEN.

They are very similar personality wise. They are open, expansive, passionate and are experiencing the energy of power in its different variations.

LUMEN is convincing CAL-GIS, that they both have the capacity to govern independently of the superior counsels and beyond the guidelines that the Creator of this Universe has for this area.

I think that our Planetary Prince is surrendering to the temptation and wants to do things in his own way, without strictly complying with guidelines that the **Eldery Counsel** have set forth.
The Earth, as well as the other planets that orbit around the Sun, is under the direction of Eldery Counsel who inhabits the **Sun**.

These beings, work for the harmony throughout the Solar System.

Those from the Sun are under the guidelines of those that rule the Pleiades, which have their headquarters in **Alcione**, its most important star. They have to follow the guidelines from **Sirius**. And so on and so forth, to higher levels above.

All work to have harmony and so that the plans designed by the Creator of the Universe, in other words, **"THE MASTER PLAN",** are followed.

CAL-GIS has prepared a party.

He has invited very important ambassadors from all of the nearby Systems with the excuse of showing them our work with humans and have them see how well we are doing,... hahahaha...

He is preparing a big event.

And what is my practice exercise in all this?...
Well the Creator, Miká, has asked me to be his eyes, ears and voice in the Earth.
But in secret, no one should know about it. Shhhh...

The way to communicate with Him is very interesting.
In order to do so, Van and Ebanne, (or Taaron and myself), make love.

We have a sexual link.

When my force explodes, the energy called kundalini becomes involved, and circulates through the spine. This energy is activated with such power, that it provokes my channels to open up, my chakras are so activated that the energy shoots from my body, to the place where the Creator inhabits.

At the summit of the relation, my energy is so high that it allows me to connect directly with HIM.

It is like if you suddenly go full throttle in a car and it shoots off.

But,… there is always a "but"… isn´t it?…

If at that moment you don't have control and you don´t know how to direct it in the right direction, you may crash and kill yourself,… hahahaha… that's the reason these practices require a lot of training and great energy control. Because otherwise you could be fulminated.

To implement these practices, I have been preparing myself in a special place, a Temple with Masters who specialize in the topic.
What do you think?… It is interesting… Isn't it?

Now, I am preparing to be able to do it without the sexual involvement, alone, through specific exercises that I'm not going to tell you about,… hahahaha…

If you want to know… you need to research on your own with the adequate Master.

Today Van has gone to talk to CAL-GIS. As soon as he comes back I will tell you.

Van is already back.

.- What has CAL-GIS told you?

.- He says he has met LUMEN and other very important beings from the Galaxy. From what he has told me, I think they are preparing a "rebellion".

.- How?... What are you saying?... Hahahahaha... I can´t believe it...

.- We need to connect with the Creator and tell him what is happening. Come on sweet heart.

After connecting

.- You see, Ebanne, I already told you that this isn´t what the Creator wants. He has other plans for this planet and what is happening is beyond them.

.-Well... call for a meeting with the teams and tell them!!!

.- Yes, that´s what I'm going to do. I am going to talk to everybody, and tell them what is happening. This is very serious my dear and... I'm not going to tolerate it!

Van calls everybody and when he shares the information, he sees the surprised faces of each one of them.

Some agree with what CAL-GIS' is organizing, they believe it would be good for everyone. Van is becoming exasperated.

The meeting is running too long, people say that **"they have to think it over"**… Van complains…

.- Think?… What it is that you have to think about?
We are in this planet with an objective,,, to give a formation to humanity, not to be the leaders, but instead to help them be leaders in an intelligent, peaceful and practical way.
If we apply the principle that CAL-GIS is showing, we also need to give freedom to humans and leave. Let them handle things however they can!!… Does that seem OK to you?

There is nothing to think about! We **have to abort this rebellion! Follow the Creator's plans!** And not the particular plans that LUMEN has and that are implicating CAL-GIS and… us as a consequence.

The groups insist that **"they have to think it over".**
They don't want to upset the Planetary Prince.
Nevertheless,… some already are clear and they position themselves either with Van or with CAL-GIS.
Van is furious, and leaves the room.

At the party:

We are in the middle of a party, which is very crowded, ambassadors have come from many places of the Galaxy.

They come with their entourage. There are a lot of people.

When everybody that was expected had arrived, CAL-GIS starts speaking and shares his ideas.

The astonishment can be felt, the surprise. Some already knew this was going to happen, as there was talk about it in their regions.

CAL-GIS, takes it for granted and he only wants to know who is backing him in this issue.

I have been looking for Van for a while, but I don´t know where he is.

I go to my room to practice communication with the Creator, on my own, to see if I can do it correctly and explain to him what is happening.

After communication:

The Creator has told me that he doesn´t like what is happening.
It is a **fight for power**. It seems that LUMEN is challenging Him, and is manipulating those who are in the same tuning.

He says… that he is going to **quarantine** the planet right now!

This implies that we are going to lose connection beyond this planet. So we are going stay on our own, without connection to anyone from the exterior.

Those of us who are here won't be able to leave. Not even the ambassadors who are currently here. They won't be able to go back to their original planets. He says it is because they are already **contaminated.**

And that we will all become "Earth inhabitants".

With all the implications in respect to reincarnation, for example, and not have further advances due to external connections.

So he put us inside a bubble and we will not get out from here until everything is solved.

Also none can come inside to help us for some time.

And I ask myself… how long would this take?

Given that I am here for my "fifth evacuation plan", how can I do it without connections?
Well,,, we'll see… won't we?

At the moment, I am worried about Van… it has been a long time since I last saw him… I am going to ask around.

The rebels

Van is being held by CAL-GIS, because he sees him as a rebel and doesn´t want him to intrude in his plans.

I think he has been abused and tortured. I am figuring out if I can do anything.

CHAPTER 7

"QUARANTINE"

Three days have gone by since the party.

Communications have begun to fail and the ambassadors that wanted to return are having a lot of problems doing it now.

They are not clear about what is going on.

So, this is quarantine!!!…well…well…

I was still not very clear on how this was going to happen, but it is becoming clearer now.

It isn't possible to communicate with the exterior.

Those who are here can't leave and CAL-GIS is becoming more furious by the day, as he can not connect with LUMEN.

I wonder whether he is also on quarantine or something like that, because, in the end, he is the lead in this story.

Van had to run away because he was being abused here.

We all helped him escape and he has gone very far.

I feel his sadness in my heart. He is being righteous with his ideas, but he is not being understood. Some people support him and have left with him.

The consequence of all this is that the job that we were doing with humans has been paralyzed.

They are puzzled to see us going so crazy.

They don't understand what is happening.

And about harmony: nothing. Everything is chaos and disorder.

I feel strange, I don't know what is going to happen, but I don't like it at all.

You can feel something in the environment.

It seems that our "immortal" condition is vanishing. Some are getting sick, something that has never happened before. We will see what happens next. I will keep telling you about it.

Some time afterwards.

The Creator has told me, that **for sure** no one can get in or get out.

Those of us who are here are going to go into the incarnation wheel, reincarnating over and over again, until we learn our lesson.

Until we are humble and respect the Creator's guidelines, as a team, not individually. And above all, understand **who is in charge here**,… hahahahaha…
Well, He has not said it in such a way, it is my "interpretation"… hahahaha…

We will reproduce as humans do.

The ambassadors will be distributed all over the planet.

As they have different forms, they will momentarily be in different places and their shape will become similar to the human shape, although with some special characteristics.

In the future, they will be called Chinese, Hindis, Native Americans, African Americans, etc…

They will form what will be called: the "races".

In this way, they will contribute to the Earth qualities of their planets of origin.

For instance, some that are from the Pleiades, will be now in North America and will form the tribe of the Native Americans in the US and Canada.

Our means of transportation are being damaged and we don't have spare parts or way's of connecting with other places to get them.

Our tools are deteriorating.

Our energetic and mental capabilities are diminishing little by little.

We are becoming sleepy, without energy, without the eagerness of doing anything, just rest.

The brain doesn't work with the customary agility.

So, this is quarantine… wow!!…

It doesn't please me at all.

It seems that I will incarnate in human…

Mmmmmmm… it's sleepy…

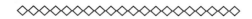

CHAPTER 8

"REINCARNATIONS"

I open my eyes a little bit to tell you about a few things.

I remember some lives. I am not clear on the order.

Half asleep and with some effort, I am going to review those lives that have marked me some way or another.

The lives in Japan stand out.

Those as a Samurai I specially liked.

Finally male lives! Have you noticed the bunch of female lives I have had... That was because I still had to learn about the female side.

With a female body it is easier to learn the levels of love, the male bodies find it easier to learn the energy of power.

Wisdom can be learned by both.

Well, love and power too, but depending on how the world is managed, sometimes it's easier in one body or the other.

Above all, it depends on who has the power in that place at that moment, men or women.

Usually and for a long time, power has been held by men who have treated everyone else as their property.

And this was the way with samurais, and their **"code of honor"**, with their warriors' training, their respect, and obedience to the leader. And their swords. The katanas.

Handling of the sword is an art in itself.
When the fire weapons arrived, all of this ended.

And let's not talk about the "codes of honor"… they have become very obsolete.

I think I had several lives in Japan, with different bodies.
I like this energy quite a lot.

Other lives that I quite liked were the religious ones.

These nuns and the misunderstood, sad, and martyred eager priests that fireproof faith… I also liked them a lot.

Always trying to get closer to the Creator.

I remember one, precisely, in Italy, in which since I was very young I had wanted to become a nun, but my parents forced me to marry.
I had two children. My husband abused me. At the end, everyone was delinquent and died one way or another.

Finally widowed, without parents, or children, I tried to get into the convent.

But there were nuns who prevented me from entering.

I had divine help however and in the end I was admitted.

But the mother Superior asked me for impossible things. For example, to take care of a dried and dead vine. But, …at the end… with a little of patience and a lot of constancy… I miraculously revived it.

In my religious effervescence, I asked Jesus to help me understand him, and feel his martyrdom. I received a thorn like his on my forehead.

That created a lot of controversy in the convent.

It smelled bad because it got infected, it looked horrible. But I was very happy with my "thorn crown sample" at the forehead.

One day, the Pope came to visit the region, and I asked the mother Superior, who by the way, was Ainde, one of the elohims for permission to see him. She didn't allow me to because of the wound.

I had therefore no other choice but to ask Jesus to clean that wound so that I could go on the visit.
And it removed. My wound was clean and I left with a group of people to receive his blessing.

When I returned, my wound also came back.

In that time we liked to suffer and offer that suffering to God.

We gave ourselves lashes and things like that. We had tools of self-punishment like a sackcloth that we wore below our clothes. And we offered the suffering.

It was a way to tell the Creator to take away the quarantine.

We suffered for Humankind. We asked for forgiveness of our sins and Humankind's sins.

As if it was our mistake. This in fact was.

But, it seems that it was not the time yet, to get out of quarantine, because it has lasted one more season.

Another life I liked was the one of a sibyl in Greece.

This life was already one of preparation for being a "channel of Light".

We were on the Delphi Temple, very important characters came and we told them what we saw in their future.

We heated some herbs and the vapors helped us connect.

Before this stage, we went through incarnations in Lemur and Atlantis.

The one in Atlantis was indeed related to evacuation plans.

I'll tell you:
In Atlantis, I was part of a group where there was a King and his court.
I had the body of a girl, I remember my youngster stage, when there was talk about an asteroid or a moon from

those that existed then, ... which was to fall above the Atlantis continent and destroy it.

This place had achieved a scientifically advanced stage.

They talked about destruction....prophets, clairvoyants, astronomers and many scientists.

The population was warned and warned again.

I was sent with a small group, you can imagine who they were, hahahahaha... to the territory currently occupied by Egypt.

We were asked to build some buildings, temples, etc... there, so that people could take refuge when the disaster took place.

Other groups were sent to what is now America and built there the planned buildings.

My team constructed a huge Temple, palaces and other buildings.

In the entrance we placed two enormous lions with human faces, and we built a large avenue up to the Temple.

One of those lions still stands nowadays. It is called the Sphinx. And it sits by the pyramids.

In that area there was a lot of vegetation, water and great possibilities for farming and for starting over. The population was very primitive, but we would take care of helping it evolve.

In that life we handled the third and fourth dimensions.
The Creator tested us and allowed us to have some special "power".
I remember I had the quality to turning into a bird.

Taaron was a magician, a chaman. He transformed into an eagle.

We were from the same town. He was much older than me.
I looked like a 15 years old girl.

The Atlantes had some buildings under water.

The ones in my kingdom, had one that could only be accessed if you were a bird, as the entrance was a hole in the tip of the pyramid, which laid above the sea. Everyone in my group could transform into birds and other animals.

I can still remember our last meeting before Atlantis sank into the sea.

Everyone was worried because the population was not obedient. We had to evacuate the people and take them to the new buildings.
We had to take my group to the buildings we built in Egypt.

We had some technology for transportation. We had some ships that could fly some meters above the ground.

A lot of people died because they did not listening to us. We left very early, as soon as everything was ready. We took all sacred documentation that we had, to save it for the future.

I don't consider this an "evacuation plan" in itself, because it wasn't done from spaceships and by the Intergalactic Confederation. Nor was it a problem for all of humanity, just for Atlantis.

So number 5 evacuation is about to arrive.

In the Atlantis stage a lot of disaster happened. It seems that we had not understood the issue of power, and how to use it to serve others.

There was a lot of work with minerals. The weak were locked up in some special minerals.

I'd rather don't tell you much about this, because plenty of disasters have already happened in this planet, due to lack of love.

And I am missing a memory I have from India, where I followed a Great Master. I had a lot of money there and my house was a place to gather all the poor so that they could eat. I think it has something to do with sijs.

THIRD PART
"CURRENT TIME"

Well, after many incarnations, we have arrived to your time.

We are in year 2012.

I have a female body, named Susi.

Taaron has a male body, named Fabri.

I will tell you the practices in this stage.

CHAPTER 9

"MASTERS OF THE UNIVERSE"

What a title… isn't it?

It is cumbersome having to be born over and over again.

And there is always some suffering, one way or another.

All of us fight continuously to achieve brief moments of **happiness…**

And how costly it is!!… Don´t you think?…

Of course, as the **Laws of the Universe** rule here and one of them is the law of **"Cause and Effect"**.

Everything that happens within you, that is thoughts, feelings, words and actions, has a consequence.

It is how the universe helps us learn.

We can understand what we do, but what happens to other people is not as clear until the same things happens to us.

And that applies both to either pleasant or unpleasant events.

For example: if I kick someone, I know what I feel, but I don't understand the pain it causes the other person, until I am kicked by someone.

Once the two circumstances are known, I can decide whether I want to keep kicking or not any more..…

Sometimes I need some "kicks" or something similar, in order to learn. Hahahaha…

Of course this will also be dependent on the level of awareness of each of us.
In other words, the level of love, wisdom and power that we have.
And that we have been acquiring in this **incarnation wheel**.

It has taken lives and lives for us to learn how things work and it is still hard…
As… we are… half…asleep!!!…

I will to tell you where things currently stand:

I am now in a female body, called Susi, as I told you at the beginning.

Currently she is a bit older and finally seems to understand that she is only one of my covers, but it has been hard for her.

And for me it has been a hard and at the same time a funny process until I am now finally writing these lines in a computer… hahahahah…

Look at me!…Using human technology!!…

Ever since the party when the issue of entering into quarantine took place until today, many things have happened.

Throughout this time, our bodies began to become undone, we all died little by little, no one was left. And we were born again, but in the bodies of female humans. So Ebanne and Van vanished.

Of course that this has represented a great advancement for humankind, but for us, it has been **a major fall**. Bufff… What a mess!!…

How bad does it feel to have a bunch of energetic qualities and lose them all of a sudden.

Team 51 is somewhere around here, nearby. We all have human bodies and we are a mess. Hahahahaha…

Telepathy fails us, we can´t even realize that we are inside human covers. We believe that we are the human body… hahahahaha…

It is hard for us to know what is going on. Although sometimes a little light seems to switch on and we think… "that's what I would like to do".

And of course… what you like, results to be different from what the rest of humanity likes.

You feel that nobody understands you… not even you understand yourself. You don´t know what goes on with you. There is a lot of confusion in your mind.

You don´t know what you have to do and if you have some intuition of it, you don´t know how to do it, or where the things are, for example, money, that can help you achieve it.

Because… you wouldn't manage with money,… you think that with only thinking about things, they should be ready… hahahahaha… but … don't you remember the quarantine and the mess that happened then, which made our materialization capabilities disappear?

Now you have **to fight** to obtain what you need, even though if it is to help humankind.

You need **to make an effort** and still not always get what you want.

Because that is your wish…"I want to help humankind"… yes…of course… but there aren't many ways… a lot of things are needed to be able to do it… right?…

Impossible to get what is necessary through thought power as back then.

That's how you feel, … trapped in a world that doesn't understand you and without your "powers"… hahahahaha…

And the thing is that you find your team, and think,… finally,,, together this is going to be different…and … you end up not knowing what is worse…hahahaha…
They don't understand you either… and it is because they don't understand themselves and we are all a monad… they can´t understand you…hahahahaha…

I will clarify this for you: We all are reflections of each other. Outside of us is the misunderstood part which places itself in front of us so that we can observe it. Just like if we had a mirror.

The person before you is acting for your own sake, doing you a favor. This is what is called a **projection**.

This is another way for the universe to help us grow. It places your in front of yourself and what you do with this part of yours, has consequences within you.

And here the chaos... is total and absolute... hahahahaha...

Either you learn to love others and therefore your reflections and as a consequence yourself,,, or everything breaks down and you end feeling abandoned and with a beautiful depression.

Probably you don't understand me either. Nor are you going to understand everything I am telling you... Or... do you?

How are your projections doing?... hahahaha...

Maybe you are from my practice team... Are you?... Are you from my monade?... or from the neighboring monade?... As so many of us descended...and many of us are in this same universe...

Do you know what happened?

I will update you.

It turns out that as we are in this quarantine, they have taken to declare the Earth as a jail planet,… well, some call it jail some others school.

The thing is that who comes in here can't leave, for the moment, as far as I know, but can learn a lot in this place.

Here you learn about everything. When we are finally able to get out of here, we will be "masters of the universe"… hahahahaha…

It seems that the quarantine is becoming a bit loser since about 200 years, more or less. It is noticeable because souls can come in from other places.

Those of us who were here, reincarnating and reincarnating, were a precise quantity and suddenly, in 200 years, this number has increased a lot.

Over the last years we are more than 7,000 million inhabitants.

Where were they?…How have these souls gotten here?

Clearly we could say that some door has been opened and at least, they can enter.

And if some can come in… some door will open up to exit… hahahaha…

So the quarantine is being loosened.

I rub my hands already thinking that my fifth evacuation is near.

CHAPTER 10

"PREPARATION"

How do I prepare myself for the fifth evacuation?

Well, the first step is to have the adequate vehicle.
A vehicle that could contain me inside, so that I could manage it directly and with a friendly exterior with the other inhabitants.

This is complicated because I have not been able to intervene directly. I have needed my other covers and assistants for this task.

I will explain myself: when a being such as myself, wears a cover, it has to be according to the level where we will be working. If such cover can't resist my energy, I may destroy it. Therefore, we need intermediate covers resistant to energetic capabilities... intermediaries...

When I can manage directly my human cover, it's called **"Manifestation of the Superior Presence"**.

Of course, because I have a Sirian cover, which has a Solar cover and which would manage the human cover.

The Sirian cover is **Danae**, the Solar is called **Ardaimba**, and the human one is **Susi**.

In other words, Susi (Human)… is managed by Ardaimba (Solar). Ardaimba is managed by Danae (Sirian). I manage Danae (I'm the Elohim… hahahaha…).

If we all agree, I can manage all of them at the same time, so that in the end I manage Susi.

But since each cover is in a different dimension, … one cover does not connect with the cover of the next denser dimension unless we have an intermediary energy that may connect both sides.

Like a transformer.

When you have an electricity company that releases a 220 voltage and you have a device that can only connect to a 125 voltage, you need another device that connects to each side and transforms the energy.

If you connect the 125 device to 220 power, you overcharge it. You fulminate it.

Well, this is similar, if I contacted Susi directly, I would fulminate her… hahahaha…

Now both of us can laugh,,, but,,, with the hassle of incarnating,,, it is better not to play with light. Hahahahaha… Never better said!

So, in order for me and Susi to connect we have had to do a lot of homework.

Additionally, it is necessary to have respect for each other. In other words, I quite respect my human body. So much, that I won´t do anything without her permission.

Now the issue is how to get her permission.

In the first place, it has to be a basis.
Therefore, the Light which is in her interior makes her sense things.

For example, that we are not alone in the Universe. That God exists.

This combination of FAITH and believing of the existence of other beings, has made her like books by Lobsang Rampa and JJ Benitez, since she was very young.

We have a basis already.

Another element is her curiosity for knowing what humans are like, what they do, how they manage, how to understand and help them.

This situation took us to study a major of social worker and psychology.

Even though she wanted to be a surgeon since she was very little, but her parents contributed their grain of sand. Those were the 60's, a time when girls studied to become teachers or nurses.

Then they got married and stopped working to take care of their children.
You don't remember that, do you?

Well, maybe you are too young and haven't known that treatment of women...
Hahahahaha...

So the father, who wanted her as an assistant for his company, had to be called by the nuns to allow her study "high school" instead of "commerce". Those were the options of the moment.

.- Your girl is very intelligent, she has a gifted coefficient. You cannot not allow her to study high school and have a career... The nuns commented...

Anyway... change of routes, we went from commerce to high school.

.- But no surgery, it is too long and you are going to drop it at the middle to marry. His father said.

To marry, to marry, to marry, ... that was the least appealing... even though she has done it three times... hahahahaha...

Well, let's go to study to become a teacher... It can´t be... COU is necessary,... Well... let's go do the COU.

Another IQ test and we repeat the story,,, what a hassle!!!

.- Your daughter has a very high IQ... it would be good for her to study a career.

.- Ok, you will study pharmaceutics and then we can set a drugstore and that's it. We have the girl ready and set. – The father again-.

Well we study pharmaceutics,…,
And…
All classes suspended in the first year. Total carnage. Even though she applied to be Biology practices chief, Chemistry and everything she could… She loved a lot this laboratory activities… hahahaha…

The "cosmic engineer" in me shows, it is unavoidable that it emerges… unavoidable…
How each one's nature leaves a mark!!!… doesn't it?

Well, the father brings a pamphlet of a three year career,,, "social worker".
Looking at it closely it has subjects that she likes… Psychology above all.
It's a short career, it is done in the "Hospital Clinico de Barcelona", only a dozen girls register. She has a good time. A friend of the town of Gerona also attends. What a coincidence!…hahahahaha…Let's have fun!!!…

Since she studies only in the morning,,, she also has time and she signs up for Engineering in the afternoons.

This Susi doesn´t stop… Studious girl. In engineering it's all boys. Only two girls.

The problem arrives at the time of making practices and both careers need the spare time for doing them.

At this point it isn´t manageable anymore, it's necessary to choose.

I decide to better stick with the social worker career, it is the most similar to what we came to do here. Let's see if in this way we may help humanity. My girl chooses.

By the way the parents sell the house. They go to live to Olot, a town of Gerona, the place of origin of the mother. They buy a house there. In the meantime, Susi lives in a girls' residence close to the "Hospital Clinico".

The experience of liberty is very interesting. Without the family burden.

But it doesn´t last long, the parents buy an apartment in Barcelona, close to her brother's.

As we finish the career we begin to work at a senior person center. A little easy going work. The big burden is not having all the resources needed to help people.

While she studies in "el Clinico" the first marriage is undertaken, a young medicine student, Sirian, … hahahahah… but from Siria, not from Sirius… hahahaha… Muslim.

The marriage takes place through a Muslim priest but not at a Civil Registry.
Each of them stays in his/her house. It lasts very little. Too many prohibitions and conflicts.
They divorce very quickly,… it's enough to just to tear the papers and that's it. (It is pleasant this way).

But after finishing her career while living with her parents in Barcelona, she meets her son's father.
This is a normal wedding, as all others that take place here. In the Catholic Church.

Pregnant.

Both the father and the son are elohims.
The son is Trixi, the elohim who told things about Sirius at
the beginning, do you remember?

Trixi, is an elohim that has very special characteristics. He
is creative, fun, imaginative...

I have a good time with him.

After getting married and becoming
a mother, I restarted the studies,
and began the psychology career.

There we meet with other elohims
from the team...
We are building a mob...!!

In the mean time, the mother dies, the father marries the
mother in law and she divorces her son's father.

At the end... What a beating!!!...

A soap opera worth prime time... hahahahaha...

I imagine that you have also gone through some things...

If you could tell me... right?... hahahaha

The issue is that all this happens to meet with the colleagues
with whom you have come... Some you meet in some place
and others at a different one,,, in other words you have to
get to different places to meet them...

Some places are to have fun and enjoy,,, such as study places... and others not, so... I'm sure you can mention a few of the second type...

Like this life is the stage to pick data so that we all leave together from this place, then, we'll have to meet. At least learn what cover each of us has, to later get together... don´t you think?...

We are already in the year 1986.

This is the outlook for the year...
She is working for an elder center, divorced, studying psychology, practicing yoga, karate and living alone with her son in the city of Barcelona, Spain.
We are going to start the connection.
But, in a smooth way, without harming the mind, which I need for my task.

Let's see how we do it...,
First, connection with a friendly neighbor.

The neighbor is going to have as homework helping in my awakening. Well, I mean that of my cover's (Susi).
I get all confused between my cover and myself.

So she, my neighbor, who is a little witch, and someone I know from many lives, brings me a tarot, a oui-ja, and takes me to esoteric shops, turning on a little spark.

I begin to throw the tarot to close personnel and results that things I talk about happen.
People go crazy, and I can´t believe it myself...

We have honey in the mouth, it's less time until we come together, my cover and I.

But the key is in an ad:

"Introduction to Hidden Sciences".

CHAPTER 11

"REMOTE CONTROL"

It is a course with a prize... My vehicle had never expected what happened.
Hahahaha...

In the meantime I can't be inside managing her cover. For that reason I am inside Danae (the Sirian vehicle, the one I can manage).
I have tailored Danae's body myself, made to measure and.... Susi's, has been tailored as per a terrestrial genetic code, a mother who has given hers and a father who has given his grain of sand as well.
In other words, I have intervened very little.

In the only thing that I have been able to intervene is to get together with those who currently rule the planet.
Because one has to establish a relationship with them if we want to execute this "Terrestrial Evacuation Plan."

I attended that meeting with my Ardaimba's body, which is the Solar vehicle. Therefore, it's the adequate one for that dimension. They can't see Danae, they may only sense that it is there, so... I get into Danae and she is inside of Ardaimba...

That's as far as I can go.

The rest is a connection from the exterior.

In other words, Ardaimba connects to Susi as when you have a remote control car.

And at the beginning, not even that.
Because preparing the car and its remote control is also required, so this can work.

Let's see how we prepare the controls and the car to make this function.

Currently Susi, like any other human being, is ruled by her instincts and takes all her experiences from all her lives into an ethereal vessel.
This vessel is called: the "Presence", or "I Am", the "Superior Vehicle"... and other similar names, depending on the esoteric school.
It is like a great central computer, to which you have been transferring data: physical, ethereal, emotional and mental from each incarnation.

This data´s purpose is to pass the "final exam".
When we are finally able to leave this place... we will be examined to check if we have become Masters in: Love, Wisdom and Power. Hahahahaha...

I was telling you about the meeting with the Planetary Hierarchy... let's not deviate from subject.

Well, on that meeting I asked that the vehicle that has to execute this evacuation, had a series of requisites.

I need to be able to handle it, directly.

In order to do that, I have to first have permission to do so, because it goes beyond all human applicable norms… Oh boy!!!… How many permissions in the Universe!!!… Permission for this, permission for that… and you complain!… hahahahaha

Also I need the body to resist the energy that I am going to emit from its interior.

It will be very difficult for me to steer it, I also will need training to do so. So that you can understand me, imagine you wearing some thin gloves, then on top some that are a little bit thicker and on top of those some that are very thick.
Dealing with all this is like having an ancient scuba diving suit with a diving dress and everything… If it is already difficult to move inside the water, it would be harder in a suit that weighs a ton.

The minds are also very different and I want for my thoughts to appear in Susi's mind.

That is another big difficulty.

I want her to obey me, and not do whatever she wants, but what I'm interested in her doing.
That she allows herself to be handled, and not to resist.

Just imagine that you are wearing a scuba diving suit and when you want to turn right, the suit makes you turn left. I'm not interested in that at all. Really..

So I need a body, these and a few other premises.

But these two are the most important, to obey me and resist my energy.
Without these, we can´t do anything at all… hahahahahaha…

The Planetary Hierarchy has put in the hands of experts the tailoring of this vehicle which goes beyond the normal human.
They are in charge of preparing one of its components and we will prepare the component that corresponds to us, also adapting to the circumstances.

Let us prepare … With my creative and imaginative mind, I will figure out what I have to invent so that my human body is able to connect to my elohimic one.

For you to know how we've done it… hahahahahaha… you need to continue reading…

Let's see where we were…

Summer of 87

My two friends students of psychology and myself, were registered at the course that I told you "Introduction to Hidden Sciences".

They are elohims from mi monad, of course!… Therefore we are coming together… hahahah…
And above all the "practices teams"…

Given that this life is alrcady the stage for gather data to exit all together, we need to meet along the way.
At least to see which cover each one has, to then get together… don't you think so?…

Let's see... let's see... where we are.

Oh yes, summer of 87.

At the job: intensive workday, which means, free afternoon.
The baby is with his grandparents on vacation.
And a course on Thursday afternoons... "Introduction to Hidden Sciences".

At the course many of us acted.

In the human level, there are seven women of a similar age.
In the invisible part, the angels, guides and other beings that inhabit that part of the world.
Some like me, are special guests. I am still in Ardaimba's vehicle, I will stop repeating it, because I guess you have already learned about it.

The teacher is a girl who has already experience in the esoteric world and has as a mission awakening those of us who are very asleep and lazy, even though inside of us exists the wish of different connections.

I, just like as Susi, am very expectant. I only have inside my brain the book records of JJ Benitez, Lobsang Rampa and what my neighbor has taught me about tarot and other things.

So when she talks about chakras, pendants, energies,... My Susi mind begins to open up.
Ardaimba is very happy with the opening.

And I, of course, can see a little light,... still far away, but that will allow me manage this body.

It is required to start introducing data and data to my Susi's brain... of the "other reality".
In this way, let's see if wc force the machine a little...

After a few days of classes, the teacher tells us: for our next class, I will bring a medium, so that you learn about the psychic world.

And we get to the key day:

The "medium" is a lady with white hair, with turban and a mysterious air.

She looks for the hands of one of the course participants, she says that she wants to see if anyone has a spirit, so that it "passes" to her... nobody dares...

And I think: Susi come on, you do dare, don´t you?

And Susi, coming forward, says... Me...me... me...!!!

Everything is ready on other dimensions for this "surprise".

First, the mistake in the sentence:

The medium says: "If there is a spirit, may it pass through this girl"...

And Susi repeats: "If there is a spirit, may it pass through me".

Everybody is serious. A magical moment and the one who stays in trance is Susi, not the medium.

But nobody realizes the mistake, with the eyes wide open everyone follows what is happening.

A girl talks through Susi, who feels unfolded. She feels that inside her, there is another person and she is also within.

It is a strange sensation.
Susi can't manage her voice, the girl manages it.

Good!!… The Planetary Hierarchy has done its job well!!…

Here I see that we have two ethereal bodies and one is permeable to other entities.

And you ask yourself… what is an ethereal body?
It is the physical double, but in the invisible level.
It is the most basic, then the emotional and mental follow.

Imagine the Russian doll again. There is a physical one that is the one that you see. Then an ethereal one, identical to the physical one –but in another dimension- (in other words, you don't see it), beneath it, an emotional body and within it, a mental body (that you can´t see either). Basically… you are like a Russian doll… hahahahaha

That's the way the normal humans are built.

Those of us who are from other places, who have come here and became trapped, have also our subtle vehicles from other dimensions.

And, let's not forget about the elohimic ones.

And the Sirian ones...
Well... in the end... we are a bunch of suits surrounding a
Light body.

I imagine a closet full of suits... What happens is that for
wearing some of them, we have to wear the fundamental,
such as the interior clothing, otherwise,,, hahahahaha...
The underwear is the basic suit for being in a place.
I guess that you don't know how to get out without it.
And then on top, you must wear the other suits.

I tell you all this so that we can understand each other,
because I do know that you can also leave home without
underwear. That I already know.

Let's continue.

My Susi's body stays "in trance".
So that we could exit the trance, the teacher cuts
communication joining the hands above the head, as if
you were cutting an invisible cable.

At the end of the class, the classmates go to drink something
to the cafeteria and began to comment the teachings.

What does Susi think?

.- *This is that I have some trauma from my childhood and
has gotten out in this moment.*

It shows that she doesn't know how the medium thing
works (hahahahaha)...

This time we had prepared a girl that had just died, very young, who didn´t quite know what was happening and she cried and cried.

She was looking for her mom. She didn't pay attention to the medium who asked her to calm down and look to her right.

The medium used her knowledge of when someone is with a spirit, with the objective of helping it pass to the next level.

Since she didn´t hear any reasons, the teacher cut the energy from the coronary, as I have commented, and Susi felt that she returned to the body.

Well, we have passed an experience. This is going to mark us.

At the next class the classmates say to her:

.- Susi, you who are the medium, channel.

Everyone expectant again… hahahaha…

Now we introduce the energy through the left arm, and make it circulate through the superior body and have it finish in the right hand.

Once she has felt the energy entering, as she has a special ethereal vehicle for this purpose, she allows spirits enter through it.

It is like if we were shooting air in an empty balloon.
And then, in the air in the inside, we injected a denser air.

Always making it go through the hole in the hand.

In other words, in the hand chakra.
An energy vortex opened for this circumstance.

All this has been prepared by the Hierarchy,,, how smart
they are!!!

CHAPTER 12

"THE GUIDES"

Maybe you don't understand what I'm telling you.

Let's see,…
You need to think that you are surrounded of invisible beings and invisible energies.
And for that you have to use the imagination, as long as you are not able to see them.

Everyone has guides that accompany them since the beginning of their lives.

Before you are born, you meet some entities that prepare the script of "your life movie".

Because that's your life, like a movie, in which you are the starring actor.

All of those surrounding you are secondary actors. They act for you. They play their role as mother, father, siblings, friends…
And everyone follows the script.

This script is in the hands of your invisible guides. They have the file; therefore, they see what follows each day, and prepare the sceneries for you to live a series of experiences.

You are the star who is **living** these experiences.
They are your "life practices".

Through these practices your guides are watching your conduct.

They set forth challenges, obstacles, and see the way in which you solve them.
The way in which you overcome them.

They measure your levels in the three forces: love, wisdom and power.

When they see that you have surpassed a level, they pass you to the next. It is a little like the computer games.

Return to the girlfriends' meeting.

We are seeing how my cover, Susi, is overcoming the tests.

At the moment, she has been labeled as "medium" and she is taking it quite well. I adore her!!!…

Remember what she has been told:

.- *Susi, you who are medium, channel!*

There are many things that are unclear to her, she doesn´t quite understand what is happening,… but she goes forward without hesitation.

Here it is noticeable that she has done this in other lives. That is the usefulness of her past experiences. So that everything is easier now and feel like something known.

Everyone expectant again... it seems that people "like" these things.

Everything is surrounded by mystery... hahahaha

A parade of entities starts... One by one, people who have died pass through.

I remember the curious case of a girl in her wedding dress. They were leaving the wedding, the groom and her and in the Garraf Coasts, a very dangerous highway of that époque, they fell to the sea.
The girl died and desperately asked where her boyfriend was.
She looked at her bloody wedding dress.

My classmates used all their resources to send the disincarnated spirits to Light.

.- Look to your right.

.- Your family is coming to look for you, go with them.

These dead were very frightened and didn't accept the situation. That's the reason it was hard to keep going and follow the way to the next level.

At the end of the "passing" of so many spirits, the teacher says,... let's ask a **"Being of Light"** tell us what is happening.

So we start a **variant**...

Now, where the sensations take place is in the **head**.

These beings move in a higher dimension and have another way of going into the body.

We open the crown chakra vortex, because this entity is going to go into a different cover, one which is in a superior dimension, and for the moment, we open different gates to begin to introduce new data and in this way learn to differentiate a higher entity from a dead one.

Susi's sensation is of being an empty bottle, with the entrance hole in the head, and that, when the entity enters, it fills up.

In order to feel the sensation of being a void bottle, there has to be another cover, empty at the time. And which fills up when the entity enters.

The "Being of Light" told them that it was the teacher's guide, her name was Roser and this was a service they were doing for the dead, directing them to the Light. In other words, they were sending them to a higher dimension.

Susi is feeling everything: physical, emotional and mentally. Which means, that her nervous and sensitive system is connected to these other covers. And all this had to be ready before she was born. She had to come prepared for this task.

Let's introduce new elements.

So far, we have practiced with "spirits", in other words, dead people.

That is quite close.
They are people who are in the next dimension. **Something that is easy**.

For that purpose, we have just needed an ethereal body, "an ethereal double". So as to manage her physical body in one of them, and introduce the spirits into the other.

But, see, they have to be one inside the other.
The same principle of always. Otherwise, it is not possible to manage the physical.

The spirit places itself in this ethereal cover, that at the same time is introduced in the Susi's ethereal and in that way manage the physical body.

And they can talk, gesticulate, like if they were her.
Up to now everything is quite easy. And for the moment we only move from the waist up.

The same has happened with the **"Being of Light".** Another cover, but this time in a higher dimension.

Next level:

The next level is handling the whole body and opening of the eyes.

Up to now she doesn´t dare to open her eyes, she is scared to lose the connection, but today we are going to experience that this isn´t so.

We are already more confident in the way of channeling, we know that the covers are working fine and that her mind doesn´t interfere with what is happening.

And I say "we", because for this situation I am accompanied by 4 experts from the Planetary Hierarchy, which have prepared all this.
The "planetary engineers"… hahahahaha…

So far, it seems they are glad with the results.

So we are going to increase the covers quantity and try more elements and more dimensions.
Let's see whether the additional covers work.

Each **dimension** and **entity** shape has to have its particular cover, because they are different and it would be unfeasible to introduce an element within another which is incompatible.

Therefore, at the beginning each one will use its particular cover, but we are going to have to look for a cover that works for everyone. This cover has to be created in a higher level and the planetary engineers don´t have access to it.
For the moment, we are testing with what we have at hand, which is the only thing that the Planetary Hierarchy could offer.

The other cover I will have to invent myself… hahahaha…
We are going to see how we do it… it seems to me like a quite interesting issue.
I am rubbing my hands… How I like this kind of challenges!!…

Next class of Hidden Sciences:

Everyone of us is ready in all our dimensions… Everyone expectant…

The classmates and the teacher watch Susi because she feels something weird.

This time we have the opportunity that a being from **Alfa Centaurus** collaborates with us.

They are in the **Star ship** and given my characteristics and the mini-opening of the quarantine, we can communicate with them.
He is my buddy.

The teacher notices something weird and starts asking Susi what is going on.
She stays mute and talks by signals and through writing.
We begin the contact with beings from the ships.

The teacher's little light turns on and we start to talk of evacuation plans… finally!!!…
We enter in my topic of practice, what the Creator asked me to do.

The teacher is delighted and during the following days, the group begins doing research work.

For us it is like a game, a fantasy, they live like a real thing, although they don't completely believe it.

The story is the following:
They believe they all are extraterrestrial, who came in a ship and landed in the Azores.

They talk to the ship guardian, through channeling, and everything becomes exciting and fun.

They research reading books on the subject.
They invoke extraterrestrial beings and have conversations with them.

Next level:

Well, we now have three covers. One is for the **dead**, another is for the **"Beings of Light"** and the other is for the close **extraterrestrial** ones.

At the moment we will deal with these three. We will test them in several ways and see the results.

They manage well, with open eyes and the whole body.
Now we need to **step up a level**.

Susi sees an ad "Love Messages from Extraterrestrial Beings"[1] (LMEB).
It seems that there is a center which works on this issue in Barcelona.
She communicates it to her classmates and go on a visit.

We arrived to the center of "MASE".
They don´t dare to comment the way of channeling and tell her that in a oui-ja they have been told of evacuation plans.

J.E. and some other people are in the center. There is a lot of bibliographic material. At the time, everything was quite

---

[1]   In Spanish: "MASE" (Mensajes de Amor de los Seres Extraterrestres).

underground yet. Therefore, the material was a photocopy of the original books and that was what was sold by J.E.

Tuella, a Southamerican author, has published an interesting book called: "World Evacuation Project". How does it sound? Hahahaha

Quickly, go shop for and read all this material!!!…mmm… food for the mind!!!…

Since the game was… "we are captains of ships which are here for Humankind's evacuation"… all this kind of reading was devoured by Susi.

And something else that is interesting… books that talk about elohims… hahahaha… there I see myself pictured… well I am a little bit more handsome, but it is an interesting subject. But it is not the turn of these books yet. For the time being the topics are extraterrestrials and ships.

J.E. has a meditation room. One day Susi and her teacher go to visit the centre and JE asks her, to get into the room. Susi, who gets into everything, enters intrigued.

It is now that I start my task. So… all set?
Let's see how this game is played.

In the meditation room:

We enter the room. All of us are inside. J.E. closes the door with a key. Things get more and more mysterious… Tachan tachan…. hahahahaha …

CHAPTER 13

"THE SURRENDER"

Let's remember: Susi finds herself in a meditation room in "MASE".
The door is locked.

She enters and sits. She watches the place. We watch her, to see what she does.

What can she see?
An empty room, two blankets on the floor, one in front of the other.
Some small candles in the middle and some images she has not seen before.

Nothing on the walls. Everything is white.

The show starts. How exciting!!!…

Let's go there…!!!

The planetary engineers have introduced into her an element that allows communication beneath the right ear. We turn it on with a repetitive message.

.- I surrender my body, I surrender my heart, I surrender my being, I surrender, …"

Does she hear it?… Let's see?…It seems like she does… she is listening to it…it works!…

She is repeating the message mentally and she likes it.

Very good. She receives it, she accepts it, she likes it… We are doing great!!!…

Now she is registering it in her mind…
But she doesn´t understand what is happening, she looks around.

She is looking for a speaker, she believes that J.E. has set up a mantra or something like it. Hahahahaha…

But there is nothing around her. The walls are empty.

Let's see if she understands what is happening… Quite exciting moments!!!… And what if she doesn´t get it?… And what if she thinks this is something different?…

I am so excited that if I had nails I would eat them.

I see her looking around and she doesn´t find anything…

Look …
Let's see what she does.

Now her hand has gone to her ear. She touches below the ear… Good!!!… She has realized!!!…

Good for my girl!!!…

She feels happy and glad. She has realized it is a message of surrender.

Let's see what she thinks...
I get inside her little head...

.- This is, that I had surrendered before birth, and now they are reminding me.

It is perfect!!!

How happy she is when she goes home!!!...

The planetary engineers are so happy that everything worked according to the plan!!!

And... how very happy I am!!!... I am hopping and jumping out of pure joy!!!...

Well,,, we are home already... along with the joy and excitement.

Hey, I see that Susi frowns,,,
what's going on?...
I am going inside her thoughts...

.- *I surrender my body, yes, yes,,, I surrender my body... but,,, what if it is for something wrong?...*

Hahahahaha... She imagined herself possessed with a knife in her hand, out of control, killing people ...

She doesn´t like the idea at all... mmmm... She is becoming quite serious and calls J.E.

.- Please, I would like to go into the meditation room, can I come by?

In the meditation room:

All of us go there, I go with all my tree of vehicles.

The tree idea has just come to mind.
When I put together all my covers we are like a tree, I am the trunk and the covers are the branches.
I move one branch or another depending on what is convenient…
Well, I don't know if it's a very good example.
Or maybe I am the root?… Uy,, I'm messing up!!!… Don´t pay attention to me!

We are all inside thinking: what is going to happen?

This Susi, sometimes she surprises us.
She enters decisively… J.E. shuts the door.

She looks around the room without seeing anything or anybody, but she knows something is happening,,, that some of us are there looking at her, very attentive,…let's see what she is going to say…

And now she tells us…

.- I surrender my body, but… for doing something good, otherwise I'll throw myself under the train.

Within her I see a smile that sort of says… What do you mean, you are going to throw yourself under a train?…

She has set her condition. It seems perfect. She is scared. Very scared, because when she loses control of her body, it could be used for objectives she doesn´t like.
Her fear is logical.

But for me it is perfect because she has given me her permission.
Good!!... We have her consent... Bravo!!!...
It couldn´t have turned out better,...

With the message, we reminded her of her surrender, but it is now herself, Susi the human, who surrenders, and she does it under her own condition.

This is better than what we could expect. **We have her permission for acting!**

Up to this point the planetary engineers have done a good job, now us, the cosmic engineers, will start to work.

As I am interested in Danae´s control of the vehicle, we are preparing some compatible covers.

First we have to take away some protections and then set up covers which protect the lower vehicles, before putting on the higher ones.

It would be like spreading new layers of paint, but before we can start painting, we first need to scratch the old paint and then we spread the new one.

Uyuyuy... what a task!!!...That's good!!!... I was already getting bored of so much subtle riding... only watching and no touching... hahahahaha...

<u>My cosmic assitants' work starts:</u>

In Susi's room, we have set up a special room to make the corresponding modifications.
At the moment, she is not aware of anything.
She has gone to sleep, so placidly.

We take out the first "device".
For the time being we use fourth dimension material, to begin the modifications on her vehicles of this dimension.
So, it is advanced technology, but nevertheless, technology.
The ones who participate in this work are Specialists from the Star ship. My colleagues.

Hi buddies!!… Are you prepared?

This device allows us to open her frontal chakra. Her third eye. In this way the visual connection will be easier for whenever we get inside Susi's little cover.

My final objective is … to see through her eyes, hear through her ears, feel the sensations she feels… and so on, be able to manage all these as well as her thoughts. In this way I can also talk to other people, make myself understood.

Let's see how she accepts the first surgery…

My colleagues are setting up a movie in her mind.

She watches a centipede.
A colored one.
It looks like a Walt Disney drawing.

I see that she smiles. She is enjoying the image.

The centipede joins the head to the tail and starts rotating.
This is when my colleagues start the process in her frontal chakra.

She is feeling the pressure in her forehead.

I anxiously look at my colleagues ... I am thinking that maybe Susi will become frightened and resist.

They are calm. They keep perforating the area, gently, but firmly.

I see her anxiety. She has become aware... Uy ... What an exciting moment!!!
What is she going to do?

Let's see if she rises and send us all for a ride!!!

I get inside her mind to see what she thinks...

.- *Uy, what is this?... what's happening?... I feel some pressure in the middle of the forehead... what is this?...*
It seems that they want to perforate my forehead.

She is anxious, surprised.
Puzzled by what is happening.

She turns towards the right side.
The colleagues move the machine and place it to perforate the forehead from that side.

.- *It seems it is happening, like if a machine moved to perforate me.*

She turns to the other side.

The colleagues with their holy patience and a big smile, set up the machine again according to the circumstances.

.- Well it seems correct. That something is happening in my forehead.

I am going to start introducing thoughts… let's see what I can say… oh yeah!!…

I introduce some thoughts in her mind that she believes are her own.
In this way I start to practice this subject.

.- What they are doing is not painful, it is good for you, because they are opening your frontal chakra. Calm down. Let it happen. You will just feel some pressure and that is very good for you.

Very good, she has calmed down, she is laying tummy side up, she has relaxed and she lets work be done.

Buff!!!…What a relief!!!…

Now I have proved that my telepathic messages are reaching her.
You have no idea how happy I am!!!…

And I believe she has calmed down, and she is going to let my colleagues work in peace.

CHAPTER 14

"ENCOUNTER WITH TAARON"

And Taaron, … Where is he?…

The last time that I remember him clearly, was before the Quarantine,
when we were Ebanne and Van,… we said our good byes with a lot of grief…
and we entered in the incarnation circuit.

Surely we have encountered each other in human bodies.
I would have to think hard about it… but I believe that they sent us to different circumstances.

What is he doing?…

Look… a message from "above" arrives… what does it say…?

"From the past to the present it will be reborn before you like a flower".

Will it be Taaron…???

I hope… his acuteness would be handy for me in this mission.

In these past few days some guys from Vic have come to LMEB, and have had their picture taken. One of them has very good vibrations… as I am practicing psychometry, I place my hand above the photo to check what I feel.

With one of them my hand shoots up… as if it has a lot of energy.
I have asked to be introduced to him.

Today I have been called from work and I've been told me that the guy from Vic is here,…so I run to meet him.

We sit in front of each other,,, we are left alone.

I recognize him… it's Taaron…

.- Heeeeellooooo…!!!… how are you?

Wait,… my Susi's body is moving her hands because Danae is fixing the boy's aura and my girl is a little puzzled.

.- I see that you are quite well…

.- Where were you…?

.- I have done some human incarnations, with a lot of effort and sacrifice.
It has been marked in the Akashic Registrys that I am a rebel and they are making me have a real bad time….- But you were in favor of following the Creator's rules… what has happened?…

.- Well, here you have to follow the orders from the Planetary Prince and you know what happened... so...

.- Well... and now what do you do...?.

.- Well I have the body that you're looking at and live in Vic. I have studied a nurse course, I have been in the army and I am very interested in Decreting...

.- To Decrete?... what does that mean?.

.- There is a group of people that recites some very powerful phrases that are called decretes. They have a channel that connects with the Ascended Masters.

.- Ascended Masters?... who are they?

.- They are people who have evolved so much that they can exit the planet... Nevertheless, some of them stay to help others.

.- And they can get out of the planet...???

Taaron shrinks his shoulders ...

.- I don't know what to say.

.- Hey,,, let me introduce my Danae body, it is a Sirian vehicle and my body Ardaimba, which is a Solar vehicle. What are your bodies like?... how do you call them?

.- Well I have not named them... Sirian body and Solar body... simply.
Hahahaha... Hey Teje-Ma...

.- Tell me Taaron...

.- Now that we have found each other we aren't going to separate... are we?
You know that I quite like to be with you always... we do a very good job together...

.-Well... let's see how we manage through the physical bodies... if we are compatible or if we throw the plates to each other in the head... hahahaha...
What it is important is that we have met...

.- Hurray...!!!!

.- Bravo...!!!

We hold hands and we jump and dance...!!!

CHAPTER 15

"THE LAWS OF THE UNIVERSE"

Now, let's go to the more mechanical part which is sorting out the protections.

It would be like opening the bottles of a wine cellar... hahahaha...

Inside is the precious liquid... In other words, the vehicles which we will need for the connections.

Because the Creator has asked me to do this mission... That of being his eyes, his ears, etc... do you remember?

And it is not that He can't see or hear,,, but if he sees it from a human body, he can understand it from a different perspective... As if he were living it... he feels what human feels ... and observes human thoughts.

And He can analyze this evolutionary level.

Well... I only have to complete my mission and don't become entangled with the others'... so... to the task!!!...

We get to New Year's Eve 1988... It seems we are going to party...

A discotheque... that's good... party... Hurray!!!

I am dancing and moving my little body to rhythm of the music...
my other vehicles, Danae and Ardaimba, are also having a very good time.

Susi is with the grapes and dances with a girlfriend... she is a bit distracted... what is happening to her?

Let's see,,, uyuyuy... she senses something is happening... Wellll!!!...
Let's see what she senses...

.- *An entity is following me... who could it be?... what does she/he wants?...*

The party goes on... but once she is at home... she is serious...mmmm???

Let's see what she does... She sits on the bed... And she is looking at Danae... Who is in front of her... is she looking at him?... I think she senses him.

She talks and says something... let's see...

.- *I know that you are following me... but I don´t know why... but I feel that we have to fuse. I don´t know what will happen if we do. But I feel that I have to do it. These days I have heard about the Laws of the Universe.*

So...

"In compliance with the Laws of the Universe, that you and me become one."

Better Impossible!!!
She herself has given the order... she has undertaken it...
Good!!!...
Come on Danae... **fusion**!... it is the moment...

So Danae very smoothly gets into Susi's ethereal vehicles, and fuses with her.

Very good... Now Susi will be able to channel the Sirian entities through her.
Deal done...
We can manifest through Susi.
We will be able to talk to people... look at them with her eyes... this is going to be very interesting.

We will be able to be in several planes at the same time.

Another day:

J.E. calls by phone...

.- They want to see you, they are waiting for you in the meditation room.

.- I'm coming.

This sounds serious... doesn't it?
It is going to be another "special" day...
Come with me... let's see what happens in the communication room.

Susi sits down in the meditation room…

Suddenly, a door from another dimension opens, and she sees it… the centipede job works!!!

She already sees what happens in other dimensions and has realized that in the room there is another room in a different dimension… How interesting!… right?… hahahahaha…

Well as I told you, the door opens and a series of entities enter, they look like they just got out from a space ship.
In the subtle room there is a table… the beings sit down on each side of the table, in silence, there are around 8 of them, four on each side.
Afterwards an entity enters, he looks like an ancient prophet or something similar… we could also think that he is San Jose, the father of Jesus Christ… well… a character with those traits…

Susi looks at the prophet and listens…

.- <u>We were waiting for you.</u>

She is astonished. She thinks…They were waiting for me?

Immediately, Danae comes out. Susi sees him going out of her body and looks up at his back and other elements.
She sees how Danae walks through the room… the prophet is talking to him.
Danae goes to a map and looks at it thoroughly.
It seems that the prophet is in a hurry … but Danae asks him to be patient.

Susi, amazed, thinks… So… *I am a man?*

Danae says... *I'm in a hurry... we'll talk later... my body has to go.*

Now I will see how my body goes inside my other body... let's see.. let's see.. (Susi thinks)

Danae walks towards Susi and sits down as the body is sitted,,, and it fits within it, then a shoulder... clack... and afterwards the other... clack...Done!...

Quite good... we can get out and enter to our convenience!!!...

Now I'm missing... the Elohim.

Let's see... how I can make her meet me...

CHAPTER 16

"I AM AN ELOHIM"

Let's see how I set it up for her to know of my existence...
let's see... let's see...

The teacher...
.- *There is a Demeter's picture exposition... a very special painter who has suffered a series of events.*

.- *Let's go see it....*

Susi goes to the exposition with a friend and her son.

There are some interesting pictures... but when reaching them....

.- *This is me... Look look...*

Susi receives this message in her mind...

.- This is me … it's me…

She doesn´t get it… hahahaha…

.- What do you mean this is me ….?

She is getting nervous… hahahaha…

She asks to Demeter…

.- who are these?…

.- They are elohims…

She is already somewhere between surprised and intrigued…

.- I am an Elohim?.

Hahahaha…..

Yes, yes, yessss… You are an Elohim !!!

You have discovered me, my girl!!!
Now, we need information of what an Elohim is…
That they are creator beings,,, cosmic engineers… all that…

Little by little she becomes a bit more informed.

Less time to go.
We are going to paint mom and dad… My parents… And I'm going to do it through Susi.

I place them here, so that you may know them…

 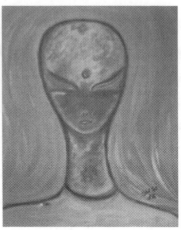

This is my mom and at the side is my dad.
Aren't they cute!!!…

In this way I won't miss my family that much… I will look at them and sigh for my spheres… hahahaha…

CHAPTER 17

"VEHICLES TAILORING"

And you may ask yourself... how do you tailor these vehicles... such as mine... the Solar... the Sirian... the elohimic... and many others that exist and that I haven´t named for simplicity's purposes...
Well, let me tell you.

We all are a divine spark... In other words... (for your mind)... We are a part of God, of his Light, his energy, his power and his love.

When you were born for a first time in some place... your spark is covered by the vehicle corresponding to that place.

For example... I am an Elohim,,, this is my first body... well the divine spark, is covered by this body...
I was born for the first time in the spheres of the Central Universe of Havona... and I have two Elohim parents, that I have already introduced you...
Well that IS ME.

As a vehicle it is only a cover for the spark. For it to be relevant, it has to be full of experiences, be enriched with them and evolve.

That's why us, the elohims, beings that have as an objective to create universes, and everything that is inside them, are prepared for such purpose.

In the spheres they explain things to us... what we are going to need to create the universes. But then, like good apprentices we go to universes that have already been created to learn in them.

In these universes, as I told you in the beginning, they take us to a central place and there they assign us pertinent tasks to experience.

As I am in your same universe learning what this creation is like, I have been sent to different places within it.

Here I've been in Sirius, a beautiful star that you see in your sky.

In order to be able to be in Sirius, and communicate with people from there, I had to tailor for myself a vehicle from Sirius.

The one you already know, which is called Danae.

So I have had to experience the Sirius Initiation System.
In this place there are 33 initiations. I bet this number sounds familiar and you don't remember where from... hahahahaha...

As Sirius rules **28 Great Systems**... you have to pass the 28 initiations corresponding to each of them.

Then there are 5 initiations which are passed in Sirius.

One of these initiations is to pass through the **Solar System**.

So here I am...

For the initiations of the Solar system I have tailored this female vehicle called Ardaimba.

(I attach here an image that I found similar to her).

All the experiences that I pick in this system go to it.

For example: If I incarnate in Jupiter... experiences go to Ardaimba... in Venus... experiences go to Ardaimba... etc... everything I learn fills the energy of my Solar vehicle.

I also have a superior vehicle here on Earth. All the experiences that I go through here go to this vehicle, who sends them to the Solar vehicle.

Here on Earth you call these vehicles... Presences... I Am,,, Superior Vehicle, etc...

I think I have told you about it already... but it's good... a review is always good.

On Earth there are five initiations... the first three are for the basic vehicles... in other words, one for the physic, other for the emotional and the other for the mental...

Then there is one where you go over what you have learned… it is like an exam…

And finally, an Initiation called **SYNTHESIS…**

This is the final step… you go over what you have done… what is missing… what you did adequately or inadequately…etc…

And after this you can leave the planet…

If you don´t want to leave and you stay to help… you can be a Master, in other words, "one who teaches how this is done".

You go into a service stage…

If you leave you may chose what is called **ASCENT**.

In other words, the last body with which you lived will be able to vibrate with such force, that it can be the one you take to other planes.

The Ascent is produced automatically when you have reached an evolutionary level. Which basically means, that you passed your exams. You may leave this school.

Well…!!! … Bravo…!!!

You trade places… and you start over there… hahahaha… what did you think?… well no…everything goes on… It never stops…

It is really fun… I love to go to new places.

One thing is that if you left pending issues in the places you've been... so drag those things along with you.

In the next place, where you are a more mature and experienced being, you have to solve them,...this is what humans call **KARMA**.

We are **DESCENDANT** beings, which means, that we come from higher awareness states and we descend to learn and help.

Those who leave planet Earth and this is their first vehicle, are called **ASCENDANT** beings. It has its logic... the humans make their initiations to get to the place we are from.

We all are creator beings and we learn how to tailor things. For this purpose we have an adequate body, emotions and the curious and very creative mind, willing to experiment.

So that humans evolve for being creators... and the creators experience what a creation is like.

When the human becomes an elohim, and arrives to the **Spheres**, it will already be experienced... how lucky, right?

As I don't know you, the reader of this book, because I imagine that many people will read it, I don't know if you are an ascendant or descendant being... but...

The fact that you have it in your hands, means that you already have a higher percentage of possibilities of being a descendant entity.

I will not give you detail whether you were created in Sirius, in the Pleyades or in Alfa Centaurus or even if you could be a Solar Being...

I have seen in some books calling to the "solar angels"…
maybe you identify with them…

I have also seen books for Pleyadians, Sirians… from
Orion, …

CHAPTER 18

"OVERPOPULATION"

Also we have to consider that the population increase in this planet is due to the following:

Since this is a school planet and as far as I can see the quarantine is already ending...
Beings from many different planets have entered.

For example,... in the Orion's zone, planets have been destroyed by ambition or because of natural causes... Those who were capable of passing to higher dimensions have done so... but... those that... nothing you can do with them... they are quite a handful... huh?...

Well, they have come to Earth... What do you think?...

When beings who have not been able to advance in their places of origin arrive... they also come with beings who have advanced,,, but that have decided to help their mates... which means assistants, who also take bodies as others do, but with a different objective.

Some of them stay in other dimensions as guides, they are **service beings**.

They also bring their angels and demons…

In other words, an enormous team of entities comes along. Some incarnate in a physical body and others stay in a different dimension to take care of their teammates.

About 50 years ago, the Earth started its passage to the fourth dimension,… we entered the world of emotions… in the astral plane…
And now, all those who weren't able to pass from the fourth to the fifth dimension come here to figure out if they are capable of doing it… they come with their assistants and corresponding angels.

So… we have here beings from many many places… From all of those where people have not been able to pass to the next dimension. And the hierarchies thought of sending them here…

Given that the Earth's objective is to reach the fifth dimension… that is… to the mental plane… people have their minds melting to understand… hahahaha…

So this is how dimensions, the vehicles and the quantity of people currently inhabiting this planet go.

Ahhh… yes… of course… You are beginning to understand something else.. aren´t you?
I'm sure that you are asking yourself some of these questions and maybe no one knew how to answer them…
Of course, if you are in my dimension, you see things differently as well as things that the normal human can't see, know or understand…

◇◇◇◇◇◇◇◇◇◇◇◇◇◇◇◇◇◇◇◇◇◇◇◇

CHAPTER 19

"LET'S ORGANIZE IT"

Hey we are already preparing "**the PLAN**".

We will look at it from different points of view.

The one that I care the most about is my base vehicle in this incarnation which is Susi.
Without it nobody sees me, nor hears me and thus I can´t do anything.

Fabri and Susi, June 2012

So, we are going to divide her life in two parts first, before and after her "AWAKENING". That, just as I told you, happened in year 1987.

When a person becomes aware of his Being... that's what's called **AWAKENING** and... we can say that from that moment on nothing in life will be the same again. Does that sound familiar? Hahahahaha

Before year 87 we will do all the things that are pending in this planet and if possible, from the others that she has passed through before, to be **solved**…which means to free her karma. Do you remember what Karma is?… Well, that's what we're talking about… pending issues that need to be fixed.

There are many concepts and theories for the word karma, but here I'm using it as "pending issues", "incomplete lessons to be learned",,, the motive?… Well maybe a person was not prepared and the lesson was too big for him/her… or whatever else… surely there was a reason… hahahaha…

I am going to make Susi get together with people with whom she has pending issues, for example, friends, boyfriends, the brother, family,…
All them will be good elements that will help organize it and free some of the burden.
Before birth the **"LIFE PLAN"** is put together by everyone, which will define the parameters for this incarnation.
This is always done before birth.
The Karmic Council gathers and evaluates you, it shows you what you have done correctly in previous lives, what you failed in and the way you might solve these issues in the next incarnation.

It shows you those who will be your parents, family members, friends, boyfriends or girlfriends, guides in another dimension, and with them the agreed behavior parameters that will help you evolve, learn and become free.

Your angels are the ones who have the agenda of how your things will go. They organize the scenarios, the situations in which you are going to learn the lessons while they are looking at your reaction,... if you pass the lesson, you go up a level... that's good!...

Well, so before year '87 the focus is to free oneself and learn lessons from the past. After the '87...

First, to prepare the bodies... so that I can be capable of communicating.

That is called **"MANIFESTATION OF THE PRESENCE"**... wow... how solemn!... hahahaha

Well if ... **I AM THE PRESENCE** and I have to manifest...

Well,... that means that I am going to use the vehicle to talk to other humans... but that I will do it through Susi.

Well... surgeries... preparation... mechanical issues of "installing and uninstalling" and other tasks.
That will take me... around 10 years... approximately.
The first months... quite a task... then only adjustments and fine tuning.

Also, we need for this base organism to be centered... I don't want it to go crazy on me... for that reason everything has to be very measured and adjusted smoothly, in a way that it is bearable.

In the second place Taaron...
My great friend!...
We are going to be a couple... we will live together and he is going to help me in this process.
He has a lot of **faith** and **understanding** and he will cheer me when I doubt myself.

How good that he has come!
He is 12 years younger in his physical body than me, but I guess that won´t be a problem.

More things…
We are going to search people who came with me…
In this task, my angels (I have a group for each dimension… great guides)… will have to help me look for them.

And as we start running into each other…

There will be a lot of **affinity**… if we have had a good time together.

Or **rejection** too, it depends on whether we have tortured or killed each other in a previous life… or things like that… not funny at all… hahahahaha…
If we feel rejection, but still have to do things together, …
The rejection won't help at all… We will be together even though it is not pleasant…hahahaha… That's the way some couples live…they come together for a mission… but they don't stand each other… Oh well…

How we are going to meet…?… what will be the excuse…?

OK… well… in 1990 an entity from Sirius will come, which will be channelled by Susi and we are going to try for it to accompany us for the longest time possible.
This entity is going to teach.
We will look for an expert and his instruction will be very valuable.
I will travel with Him through the whole planet, where the colleagues might be, in order to find them.
Another issue… now that we talk about the Sirius entity.

I have to join High Frequency Beings to be channelled by Susi and in this way, these entities will be capable of talking to humans, teach them and explain events to them, etc,,,

I believe that both sides are wishing to relate to each other. Because the quarantine still prevents doing it in a more direct way. Well... I'm here for this, it's my job, that they can get together and talk to each other... those of "above" with those from "below"...
And I am in the middle... hahahahaha... as usual... that's the reason why I am called "Tejemaneje"... Because I get involved in everywhere...
I am a bold... hahahaha...

I will also do this with my angels.
There are people who are angels incarnated on Earth to help. They also need help and consolation for themselves, because they are exhausted for sure,,, hahahaha...

Others need spiritual counseling... so... to relate with other people's angels...

Uyy... I think that I will like this very much... the angels are wonderful beings... specially those little ones, cherubim... how funny they are...
And the big ones... wise... what a teaching!!...
Such good counsel.

And more things that I have to do...
Let's see...
Oh yes!!!...
As I meet the personnel, we will have to do some tasks...
For example irradiate places... To take Light to those places that the Planetary Hierarchy designates.

Let's remember that when we entered in here, we placed ourselves under their power.

They rule the subtle side of this planet and tell us what they need and how we can help with our energies.

The descendent beings are like acupuncture needles. We have the feet nailed on the ground, but the antenna set in the sky,... hahahaha...

This means that we bring high energies from the center of this universe to the Earth, this is one of our contributions.

We have to work with the planet and the beings who inhabit it.

We help in their evolution. Mainly, that it happens more quickly.

Amongst all, we try to build **"CRITICAL MASS"**, which means... that a set quantity of energy is needed to jump to the next evolutionary level.

It is like filling a glass, but when it is full, it floods.

The quantity that fits in the glass when it is full, is the critical mass...

In other words, with a set amount the glass fills up and that's it... you have it full already. Hahahahaha...

CHAPTER 20

"THE FINAL STRETCH"

The previous stage is over and we arrived to 2012.

I have already done all the things mentioned so far.

I married Taaron, I formed groups of people, I made sessions and courses with the Sirius entity. I recorded tapes with his teachings and wrote books with them.

I did healing sessions, counseling with angels of people. I finished a book of angels dictated by them.

We visited many places, just Taaron and me, to hold all these courses and sessions, as well as with the group to comply with our tasks...
Hey, we have travelled... Bufff...

We fulfilled all the missions assigned by the Planetary Hierarchy...

What's next now?...well ... now almost... everything is done...
But...
We have not reached everyone ... impossible...

But…
Now we have more modern systems…
A webpage, cell phones, Skype, Facebook, Messenger,……
ways to meet others and reach them are not lacking…
On that we are… very modern…

So…

With the entities of Light everything is done as well, I have connected and they have passed through the channel. They have said what they wanted to say. And the channel has been impeccable.
(Which is very important).

What is my objective when writing this book?… well… that you can understand things better… that you understand why you are here and why these things happen to you… if I achieve this… good,,, otherwise… you can ask me through this modern means,… I am here to help you… I can give you some ideas.

For sure if you search for Susi Calvo o for the "Plan Maestro", you will find me, that's what Google is for… isn't it?

If not, remember, that all of us who came together, in the end, will leave together and we will laugh a lot of all the anecdotes we went through…

How are we going to leave?
Some will leave the body and go to other planets, others will ascend, others will gather to help from this or from other planes. Who cares!…

There's a lot to do, the important part is teamwork. Don't you think so?

Here in this planet, no one will stay because the planet itself which we will think of as a Being, as an entity, also evolves, it changes dimension,... and it is its time already...wow!!!

But adequate planets have been prepared for us to inhabit...

For example: **"THE DOME OF VENUS".**

This is a planet with similar characteristics to the Earth's.
The inhabitants will have their own houses.
We will take them in ships and once we get there we will give them all kinds of support.

In the beginning it will be the return to living in a town, but very healthily...

And above all, people will be friends...

Do you know that in the fourth dimension, the densest plane selfishness and envy?
Currently the densest planes are murder and things like that.

In the fourth dimension, which is the emotional world, beautiful emotions will be normal and the others such as selfishness, doubt, worrisome, will be the densest.
We will not be interested in such things.

I have more information, but I don't want to overwhelm you...
Let's see if I write another book and tell you...

I only ask you to be happy. That you keep yourself in a high vibratory frequency and learn all the lessons that your angels are offering you.

Smile… we are almost leaving!!!

I LOVE YOU…!!!

(This book has been written by Tejemaneje, with collaboration of Susi Calvo).

December, 20-2011
Avila, Spain.

Uy…!!! I'm leaving already… see you… because I notice something weird… as if some superior entity were handling me…
what's this?… could it be possible?…
Who on Earth is superior to me?…
I leave you here, I have to find out who it is…
I hope to see you soon… and then I will tell you about it…
What a mistery!!!

AUTHOR'S NOTES

I am very pleased for having the chance to express myself.

This is a "notebook of planetary practices", I expect that it was understood from the beginning.

I am taking all these impressions to the place of origin I am coming from.
I am having a great time in this planet.

I have liked it so much, that I will continue writing... hahahaha

I will write more books, a whole collection... do you want to read them?

Follow me...

Teje Ma

ANNEX

THE COLLECTION

SUSI CALVO is born in Barcelona, she studies the career of social worker and she works for many years for the "Generalitat de Catalunya".

She awakens to the channelizing world in 1987.

She channels High Frequency beings, and since 1990, entities manifest from the Elderly Counsel from the star Sirius.

She works with these entities for this time, for this and other reasons, she receives the charming nickname of "Susi from Sirius".

She links the angelic world and makes private consulting sessions with the angels' persons.

She works at the stretcher with two Super-angels: God's Love and Divine Grace.

At the end of 2011, she presents to a publishing house her book named "THE MASTER PLAN".

This is the first of a books' collection, four of them have surfaced this 2012 in Spanish.

And this one that you have on your hands, in English.

The collection is called: "MY PRACTICES NOTEBOOK – Teje Má"
On it, an entity from the Central Universe Spheres updates us from his practices in this universe.
It is an entertaining and funny collection, and at the same time instructive.

The number 1: "THE MASTER PLAN"

The number 2: "RENOVATION"

The number 3: "DISCOVERING THE FUTURE"

The number 4: "AWAKENING CONSCIENCE"

In May 2012, a new collection called "LOVELY COMPANY" started.
In this new collection, angels, unicorns and other ethereal entities talk.

In this collection, the number 1 is called "MY ANGELS"

The number 2: "THE FALSE UNICORN".

The number 3: "NAN AND SOPHIA"

All these books are channelled and dictated by Light Beings, assigned to this task by this Universe Creator.

We invite you to know them!

October, 2012